Something is Missing

Written By Christine Olufemi

Illustrations By Pedro Luis Rivas

NWP

New World Press, Inc.

Atlanta

ISBN-13: 978-0-9759730-6-6

Printed in the United State of America

ACKNOWLEDGEMENTS:

Thanks to my daughter Chinelo Arinze, friends Betty Chaney, Gloria McCullough-Wright & Norris Wright for taking the time to read and critique the manuscript. Special Thanks to my Publisher for the diligent patience, suggestions and hours of allowing the needed changes made for a successful publication.

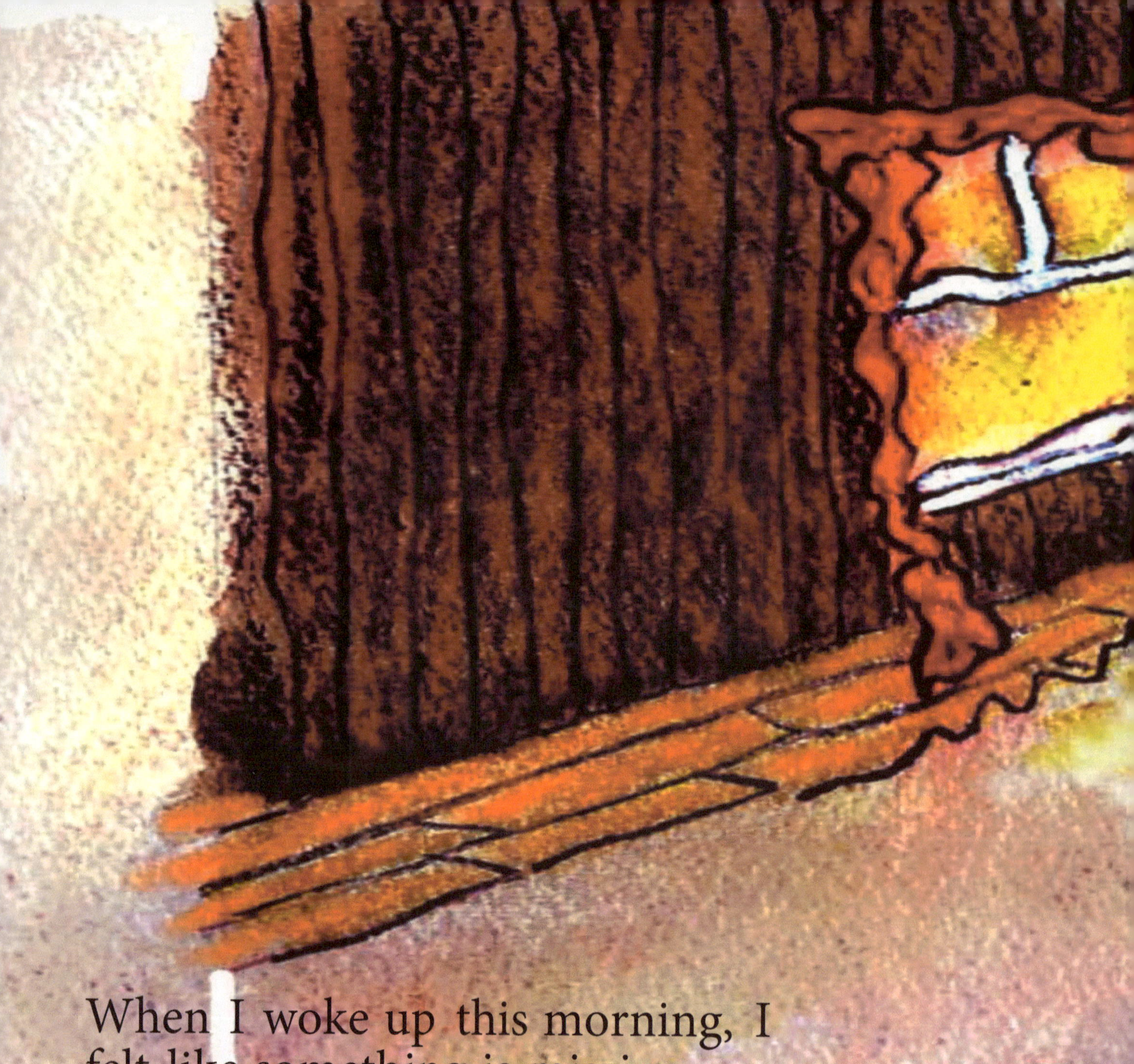

When I woke up this morning, I
felt like something is missing....
but what? I do not know.

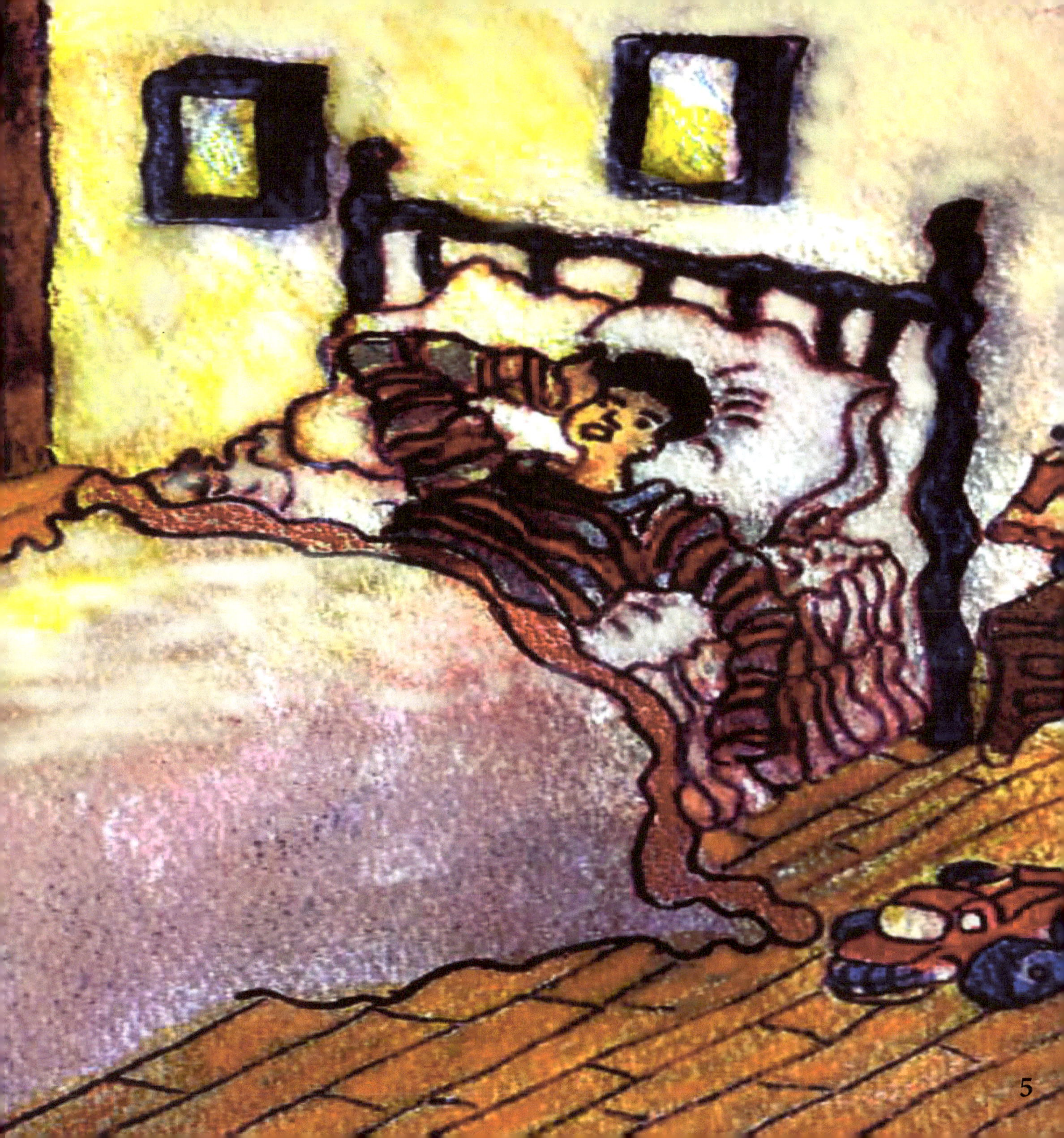

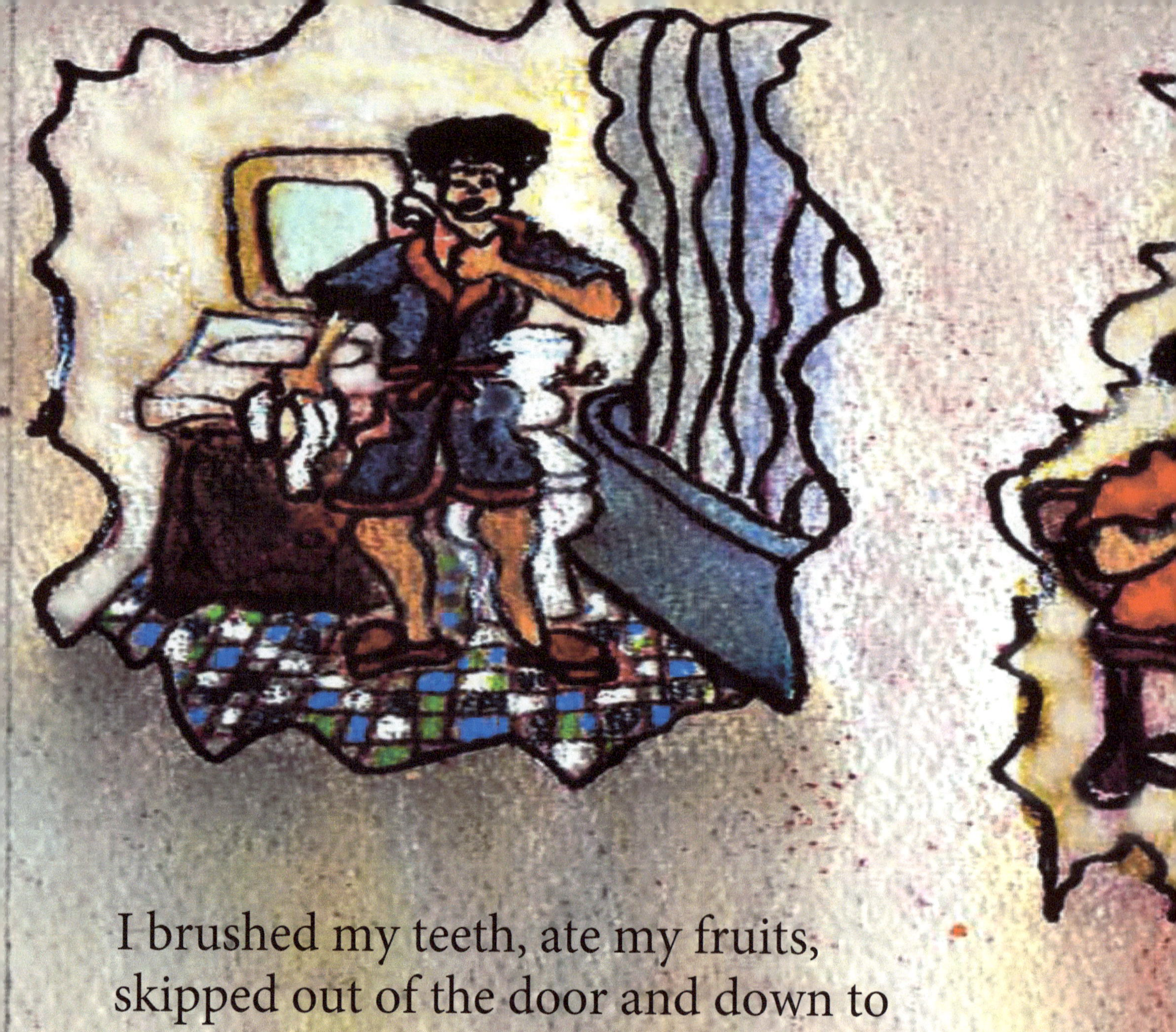

I brushed my teeth, ate my fruits, skipped out of the door and down to the bus stop as I waved goodbye.

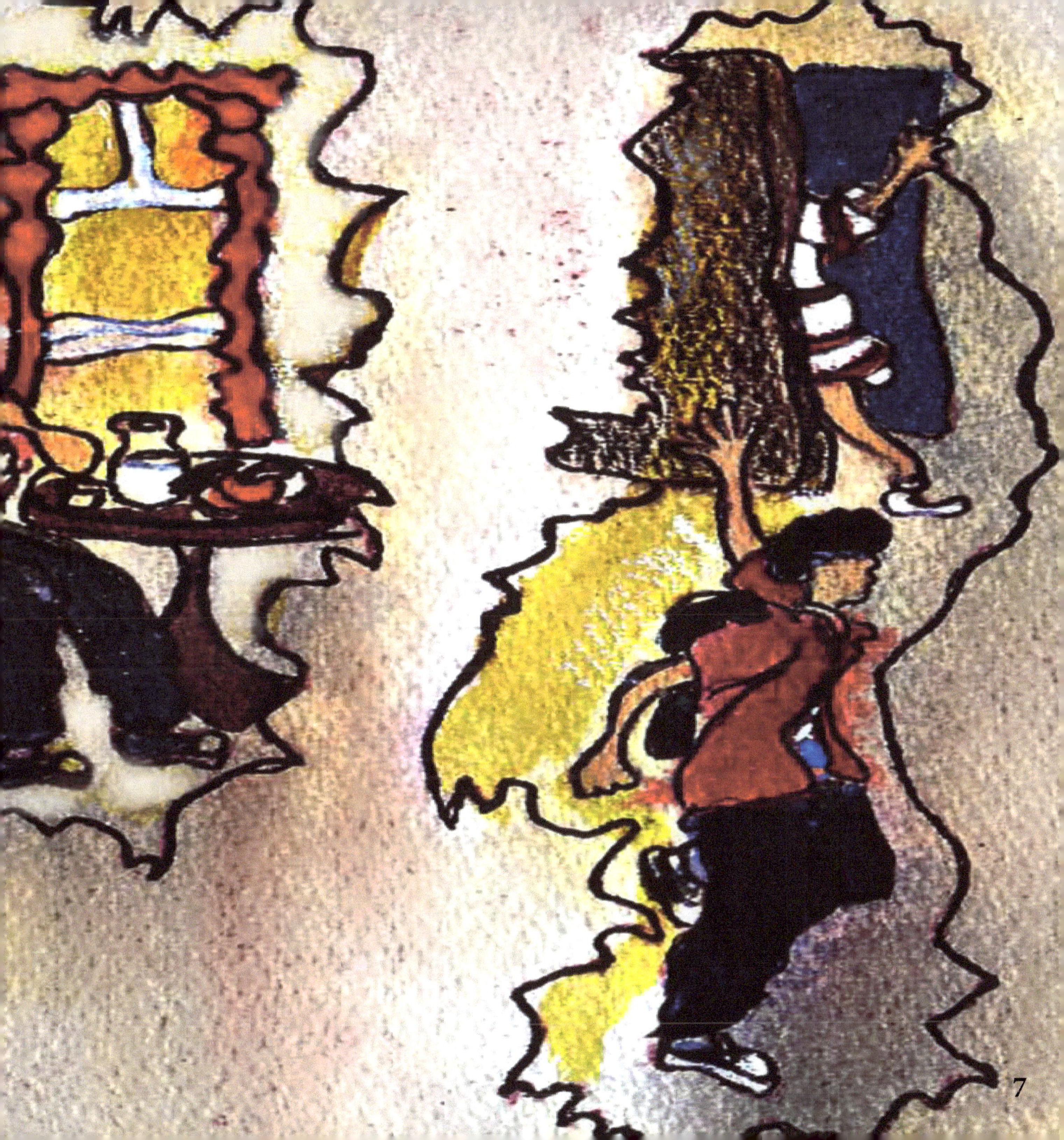

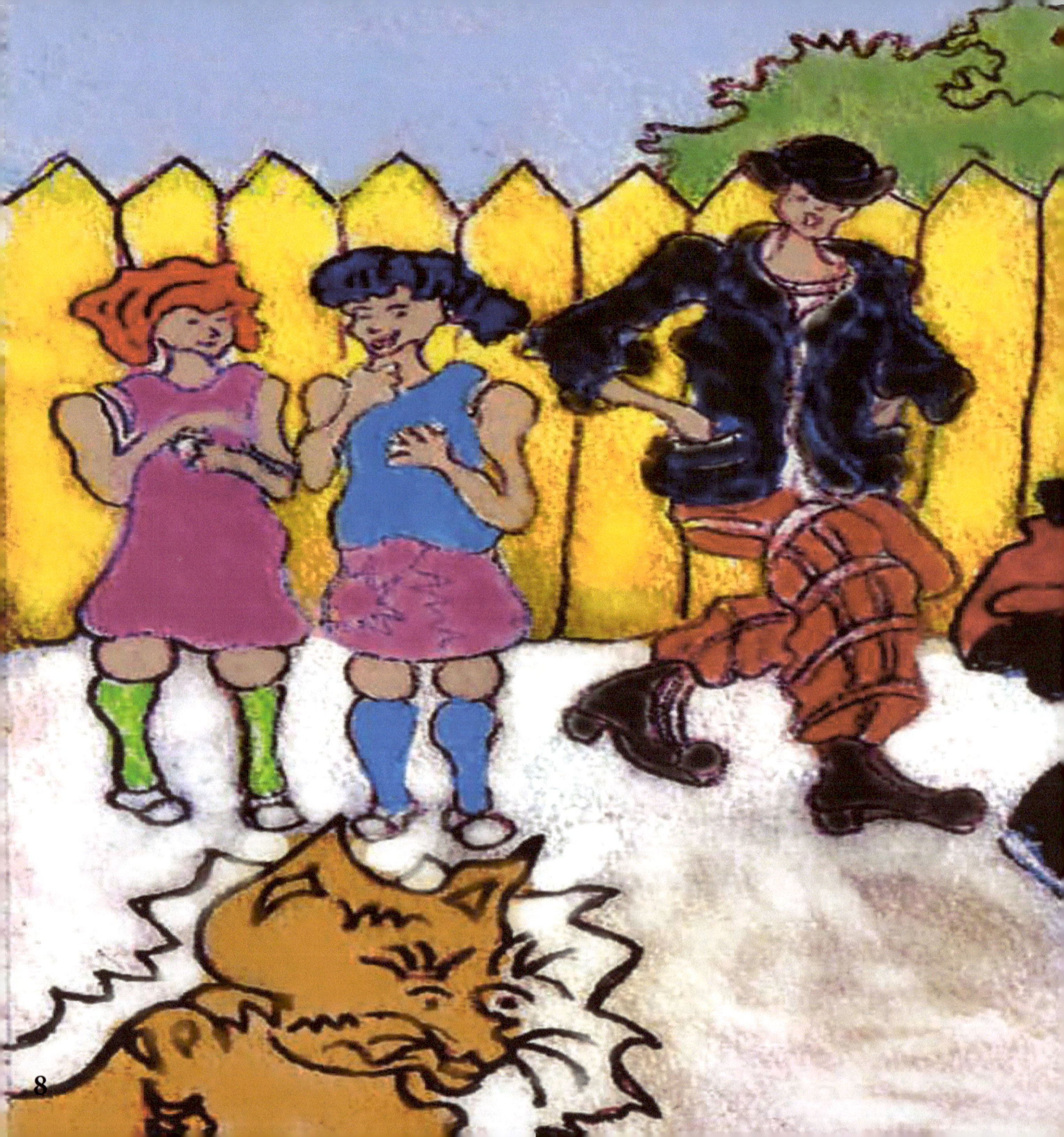

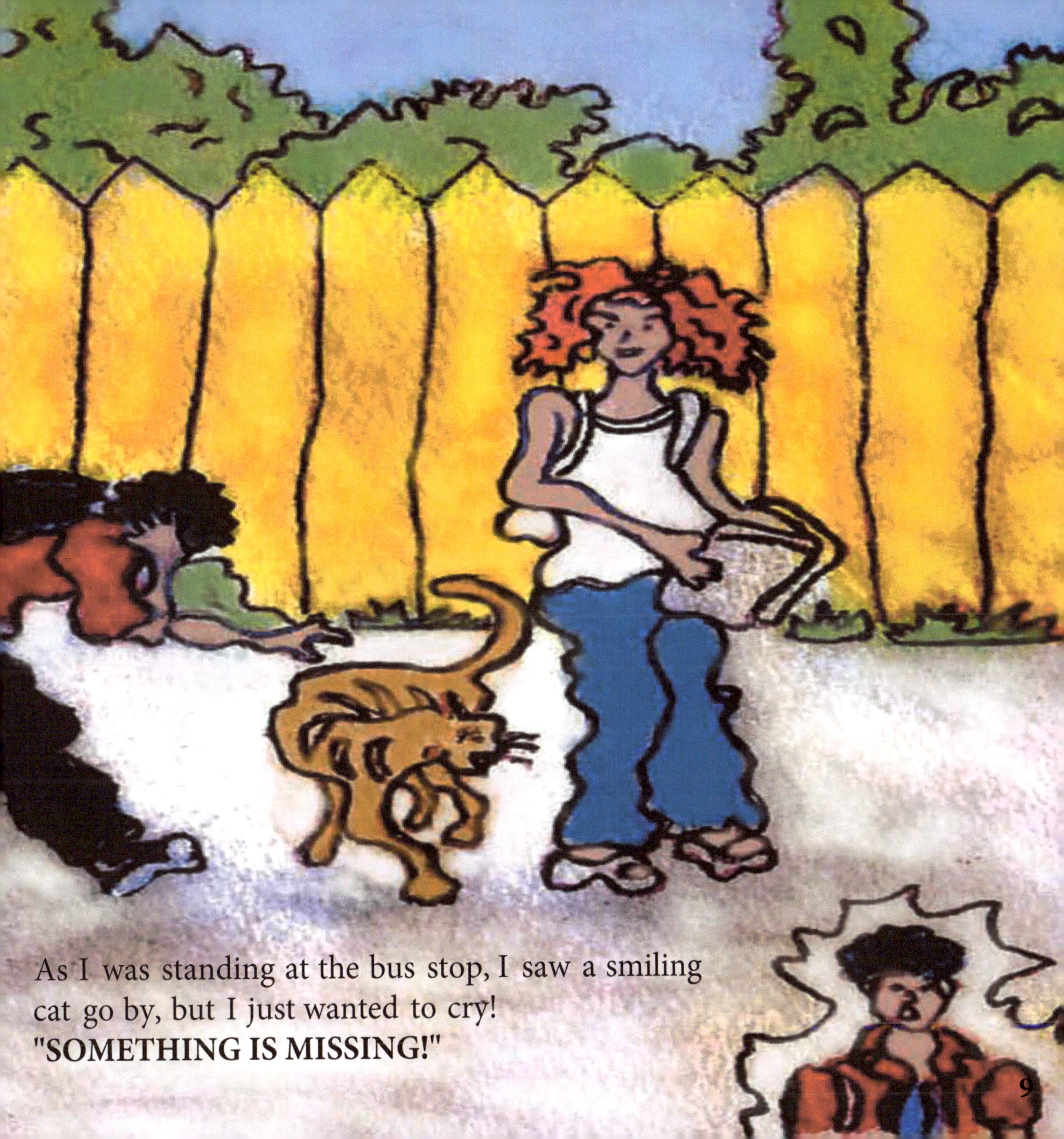

As I was standing at the bus stop, I saw a smiling
cat go by, but I just wanted to cry!
"SOMETHING IS MISSING!"

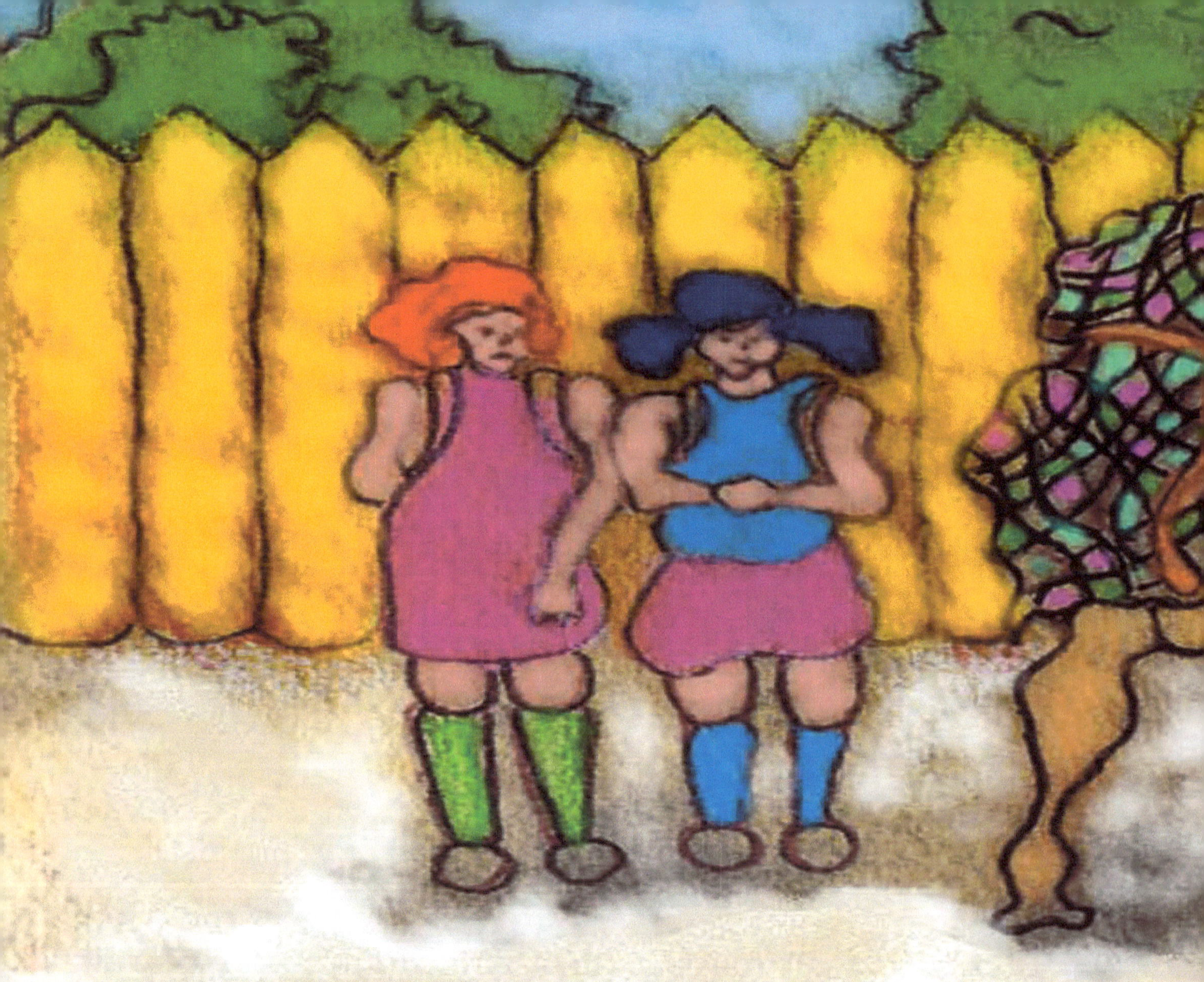

Along came a smiling camel, and everybody knows
that ole' humpback is as serious as can be, or as
serious as you can get .... but I just wanted to cry,
"SOMETHING IS MISSING."

10

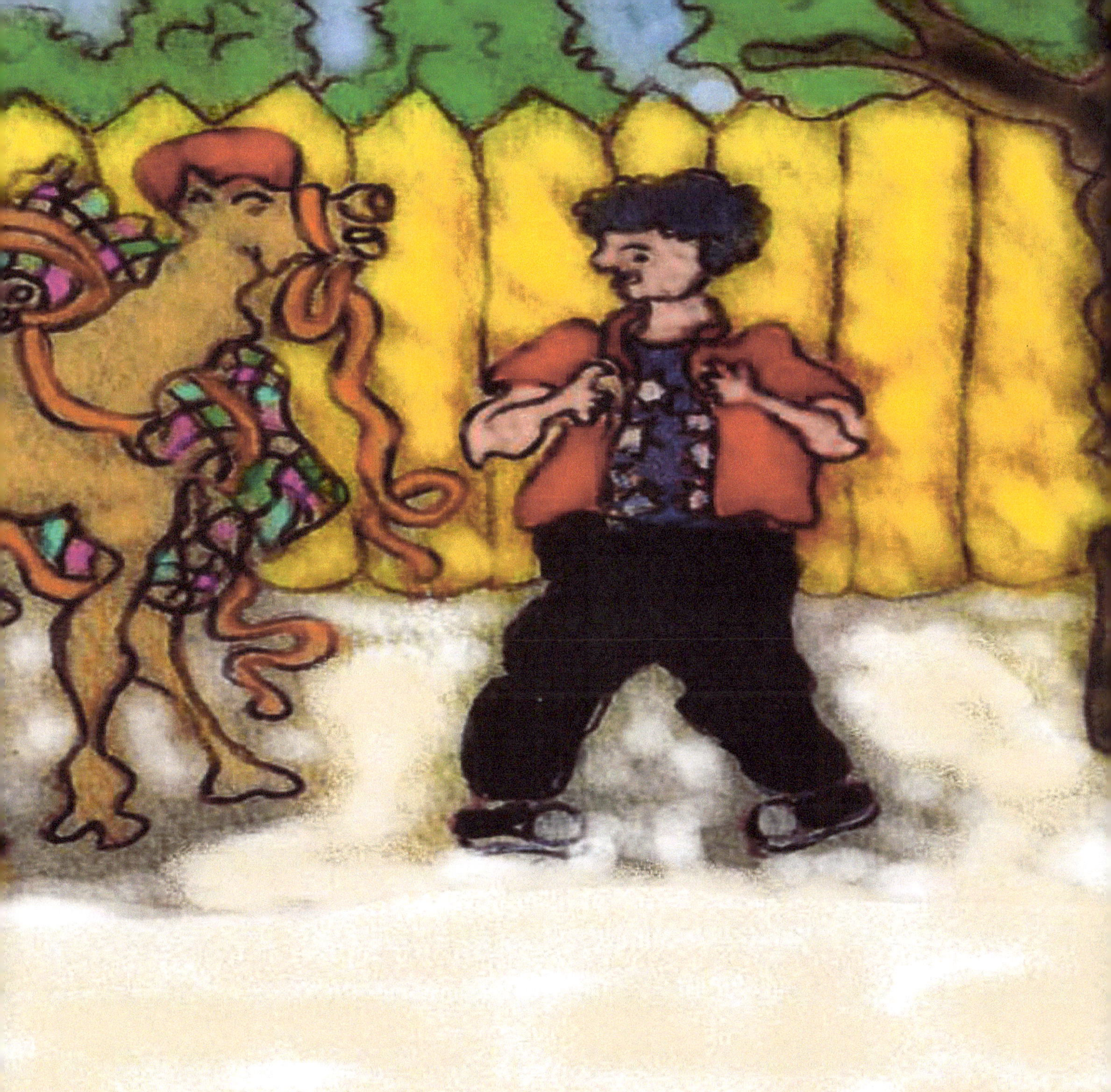

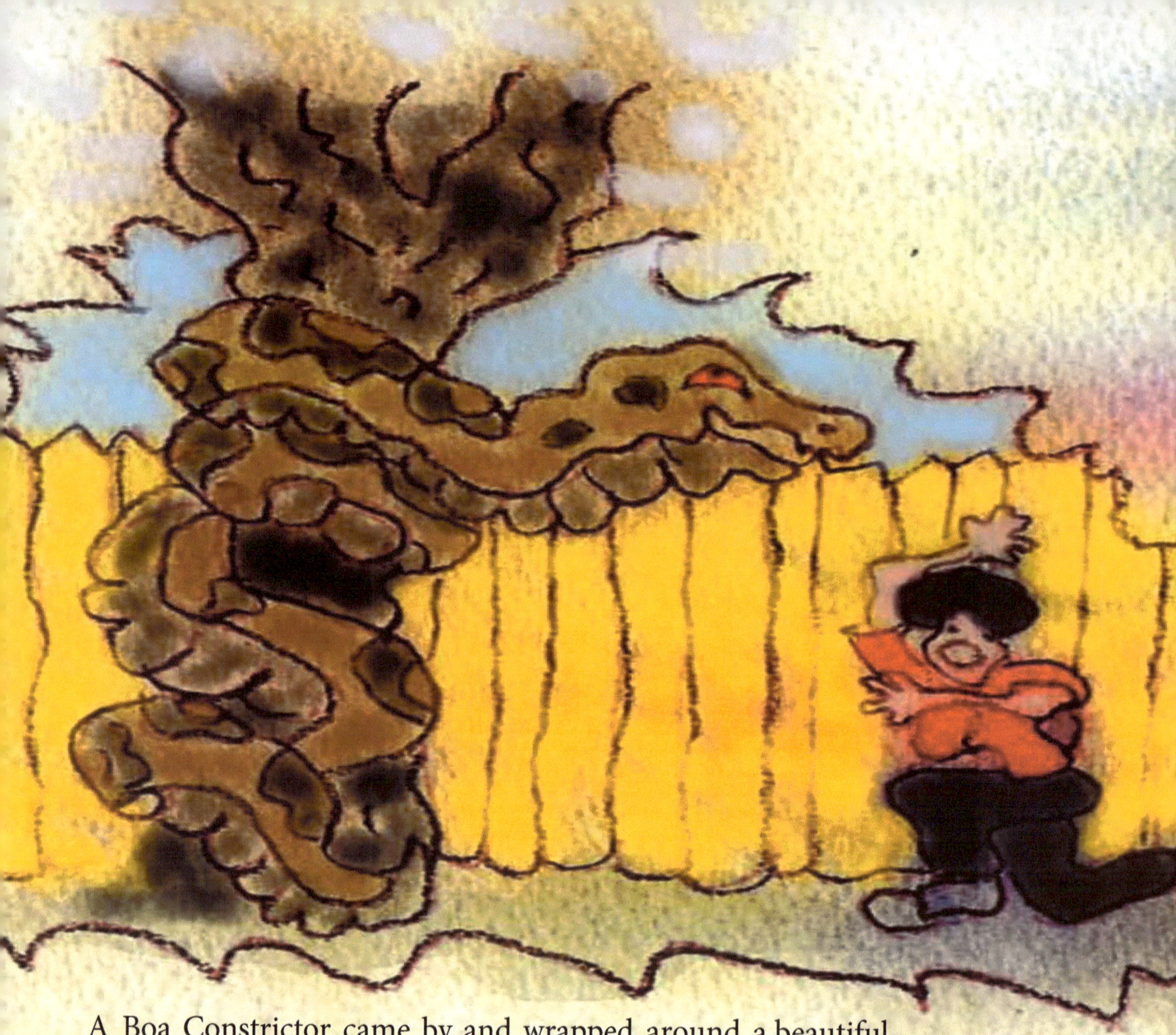

A Boa Constrictor came by and wrapped around a beautiful dogwood tree, instead of me. He sighed and said, with a smile, "there's a fly in my eye and thought he was squeezing me!" He smiled and with another sigh he let me be. But I just wanted to cry, **"SOMETHING IS MISSING!"**

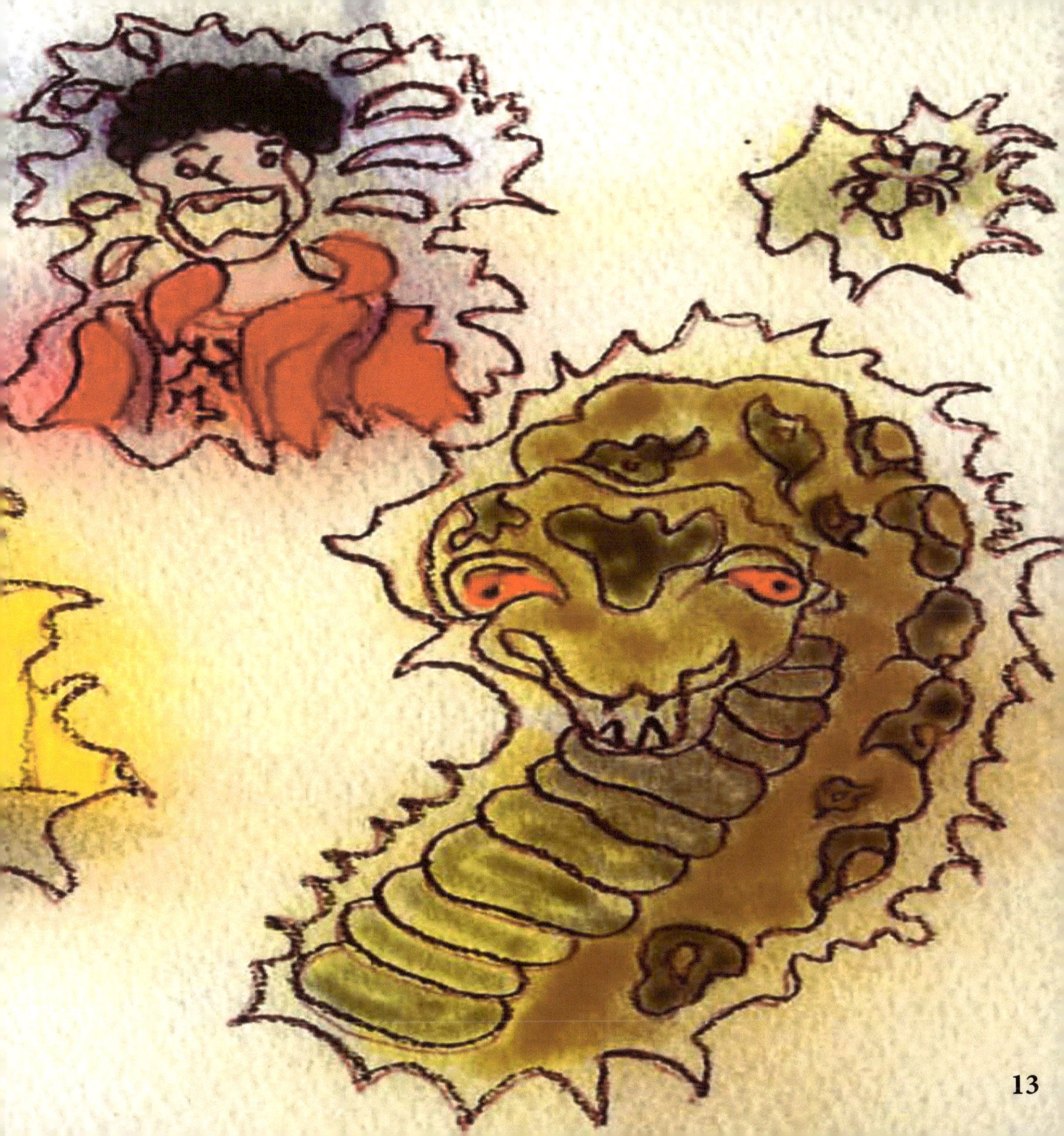

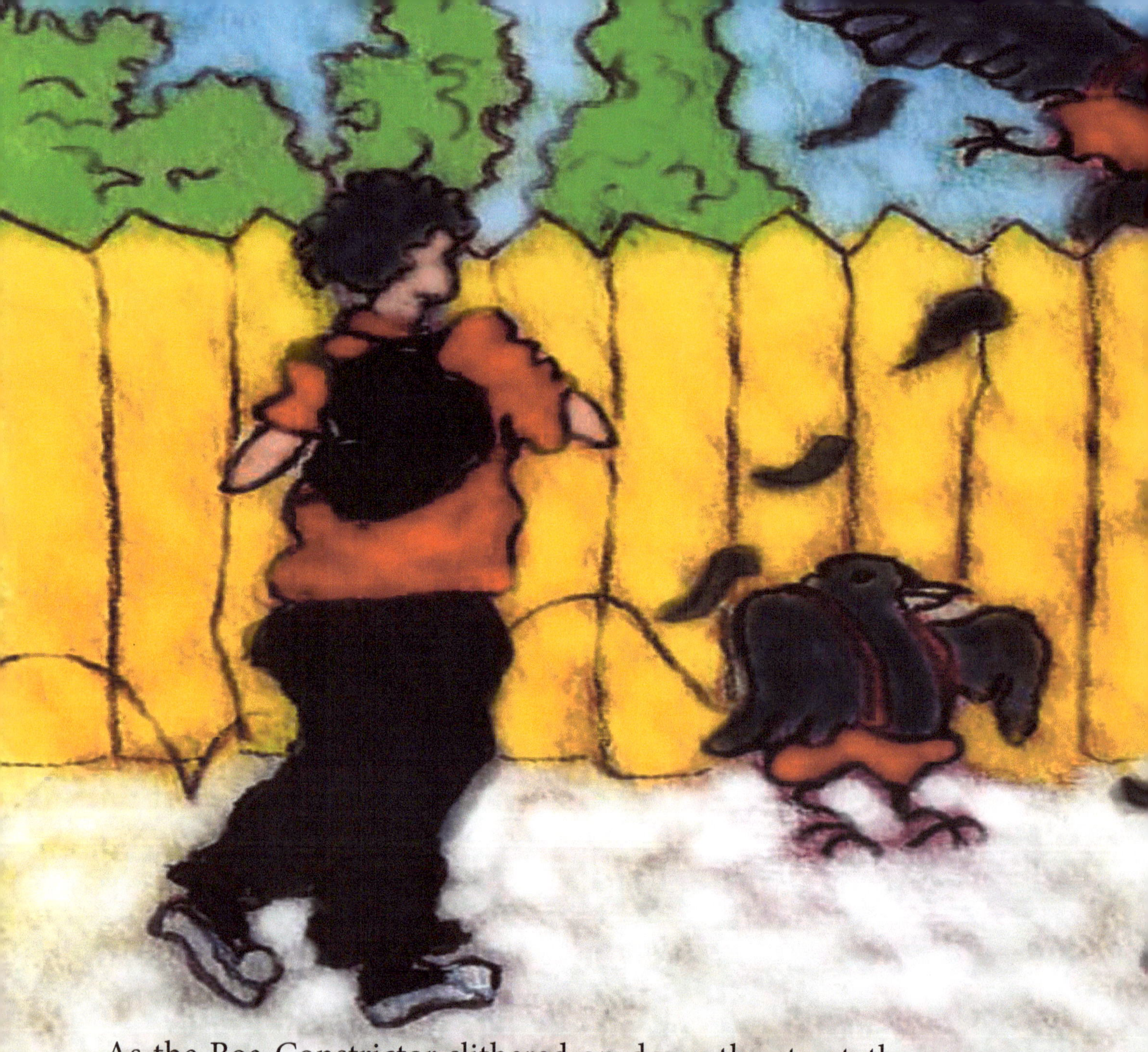

As the Boa Constrictor slithered on down the street, there were some crows acting like Kangaroos hopping here and there with a crackling sound in the air.

14

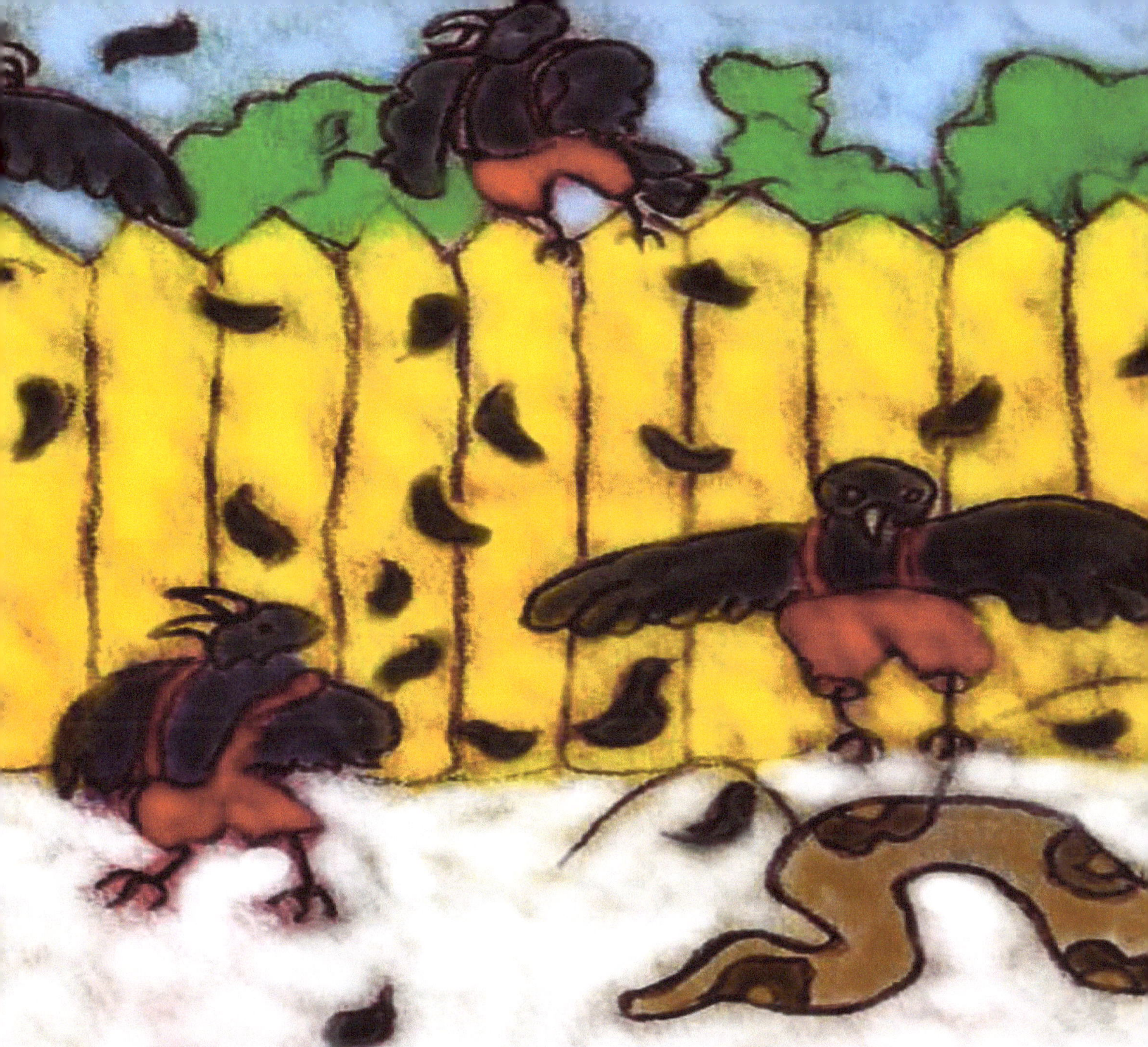

The crows said loudly and clearly, "I know, I know, got to go, got to go!" Instead of smiling or laughing at the crows, I just wanted to cry ,**"SOMETHING IS MISSING."**

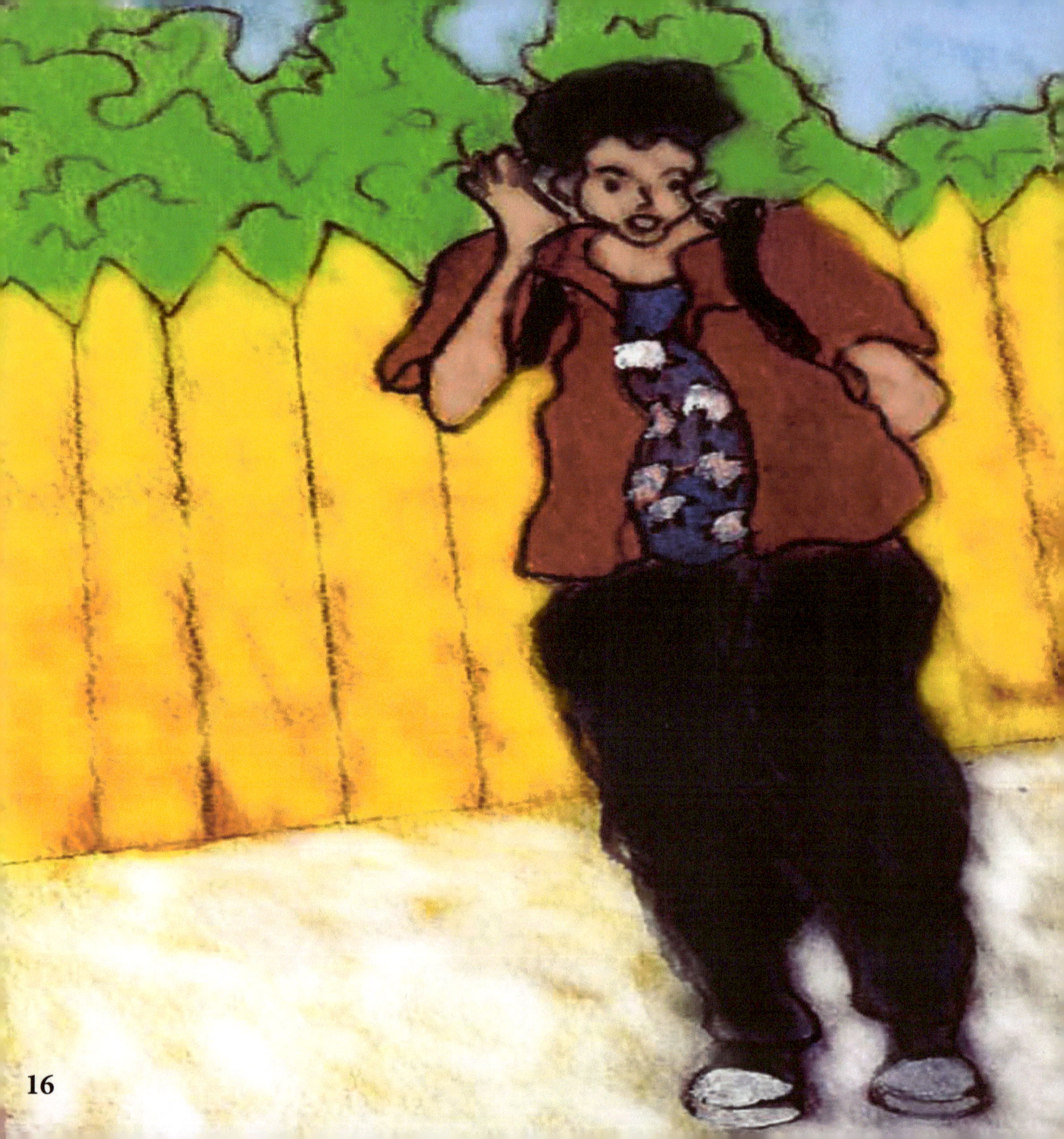

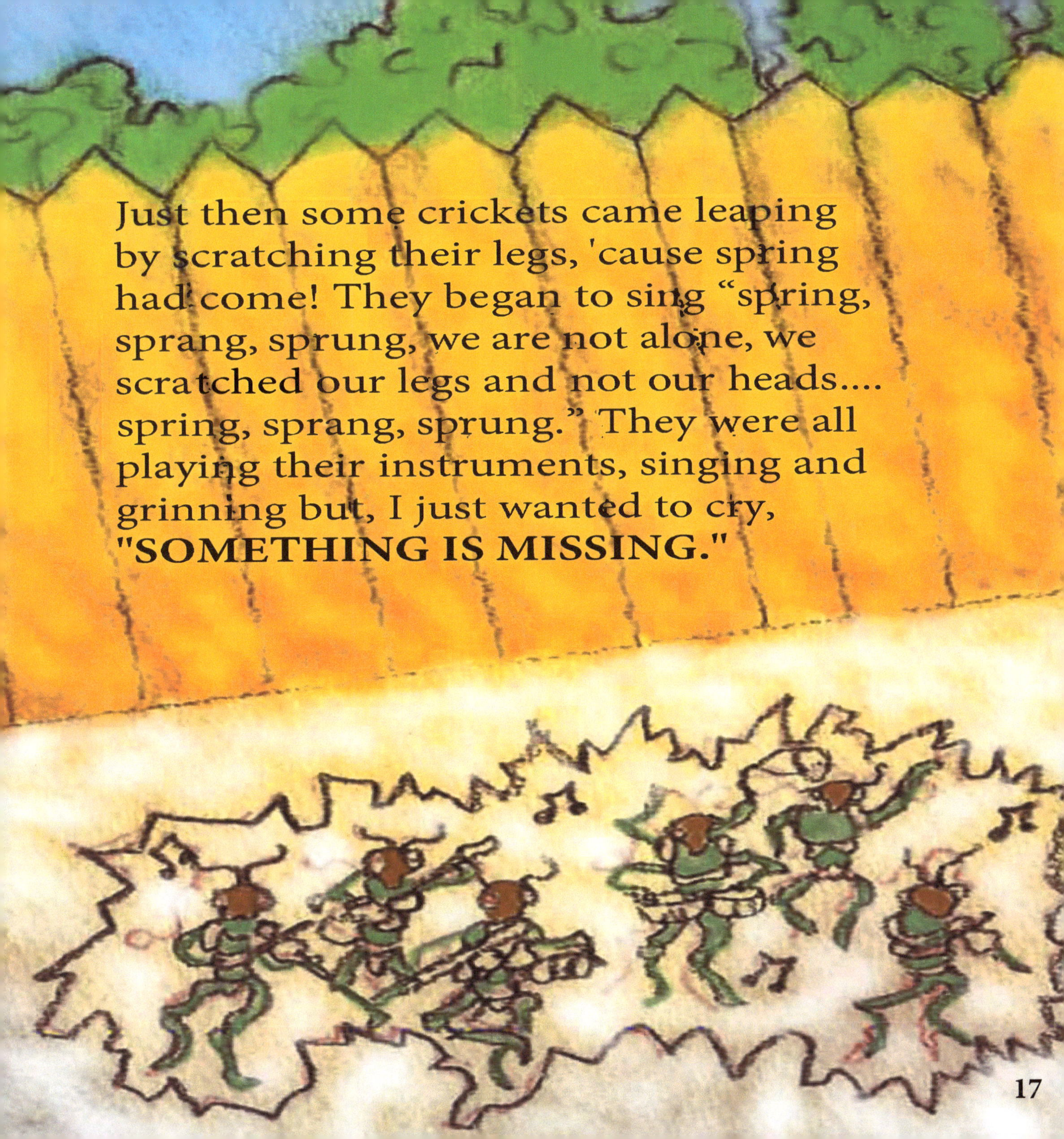

Just then some crickets came leaping by scratching their legs, 'cause spring had come! They began to sing "spring, sprang, sprung, we are not alone, we scratched our legs and not our heads.... spring, sprang, sprung." They were all playing their instruments, singing and grinning but, I just wanted to cry, **"SOMETHING IS MISSING."**

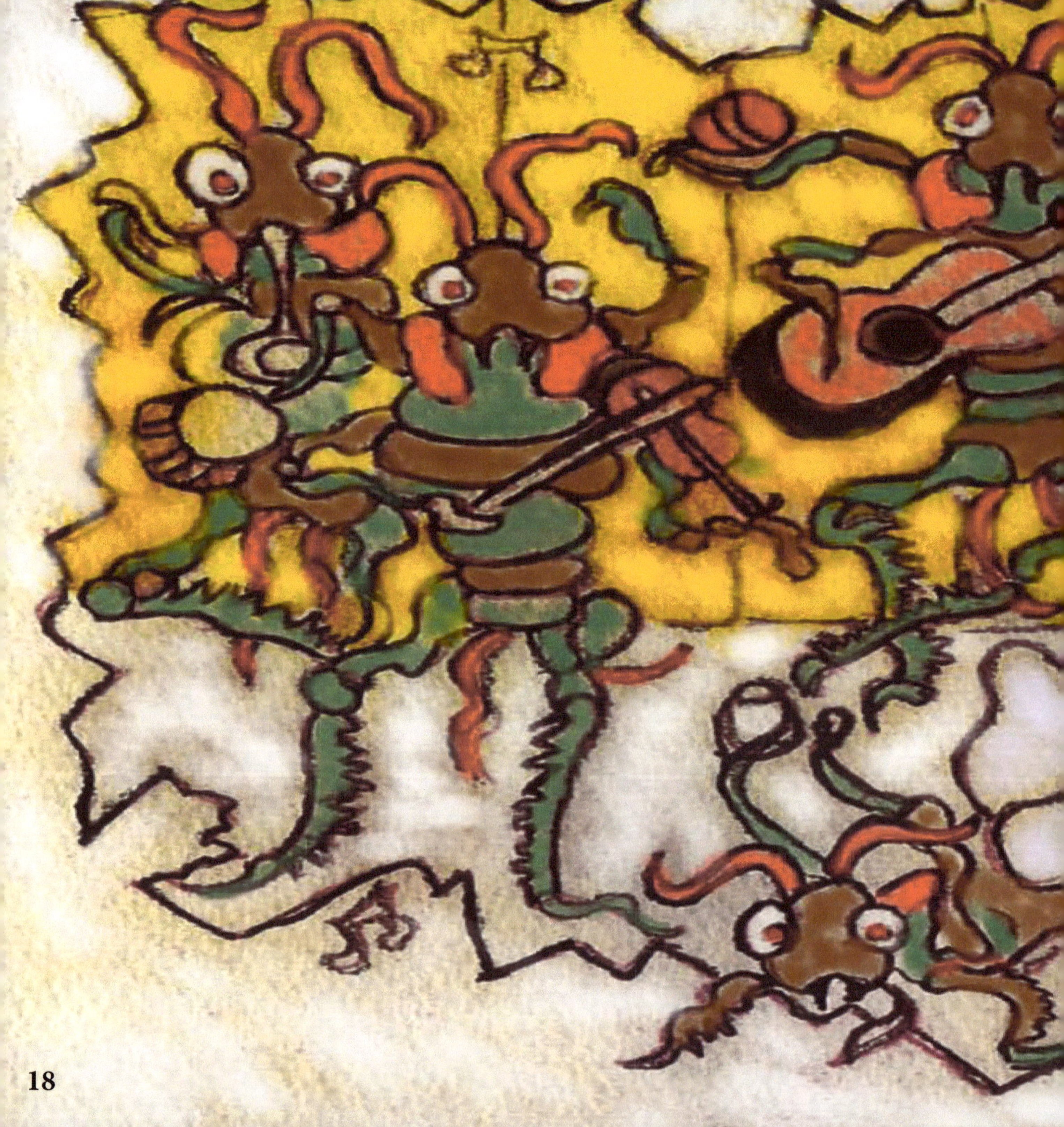

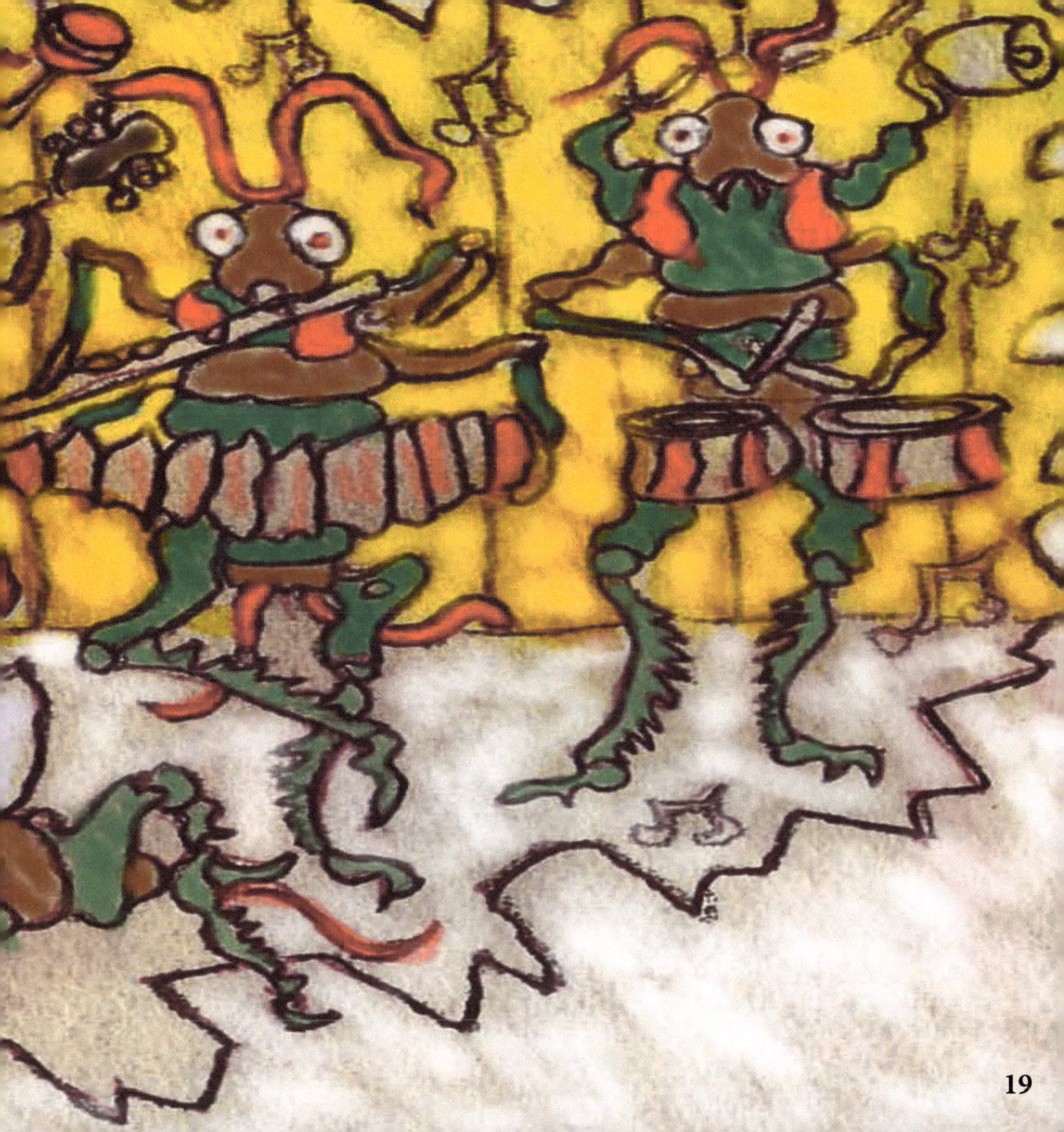

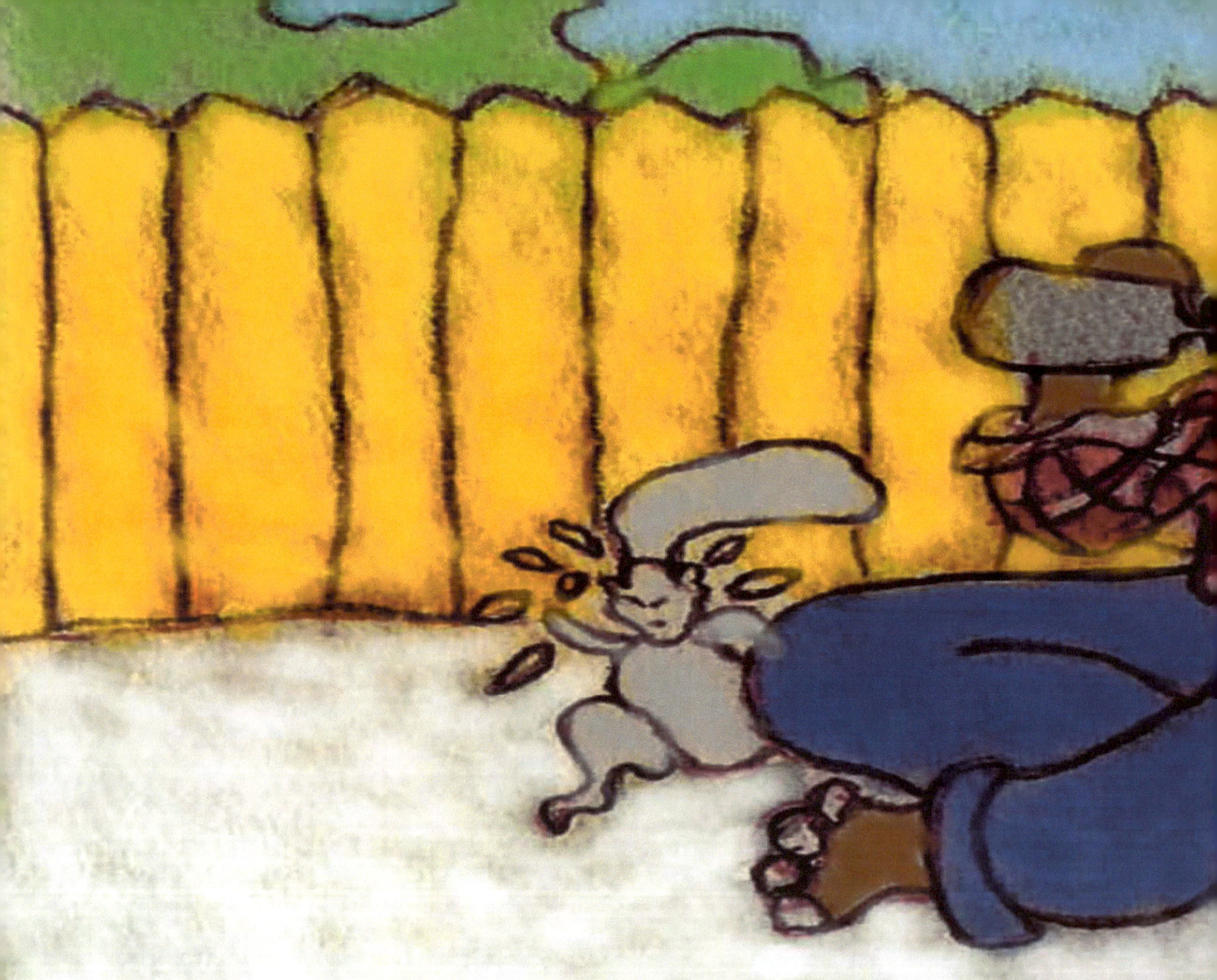

A hippopotamus came and sat on a squirrel's thigh and I began to sigh "Oh me! on my! hilarious! hilarious I could not deny but I just wanted to cry, **"SOMETHING IS MISSING."**

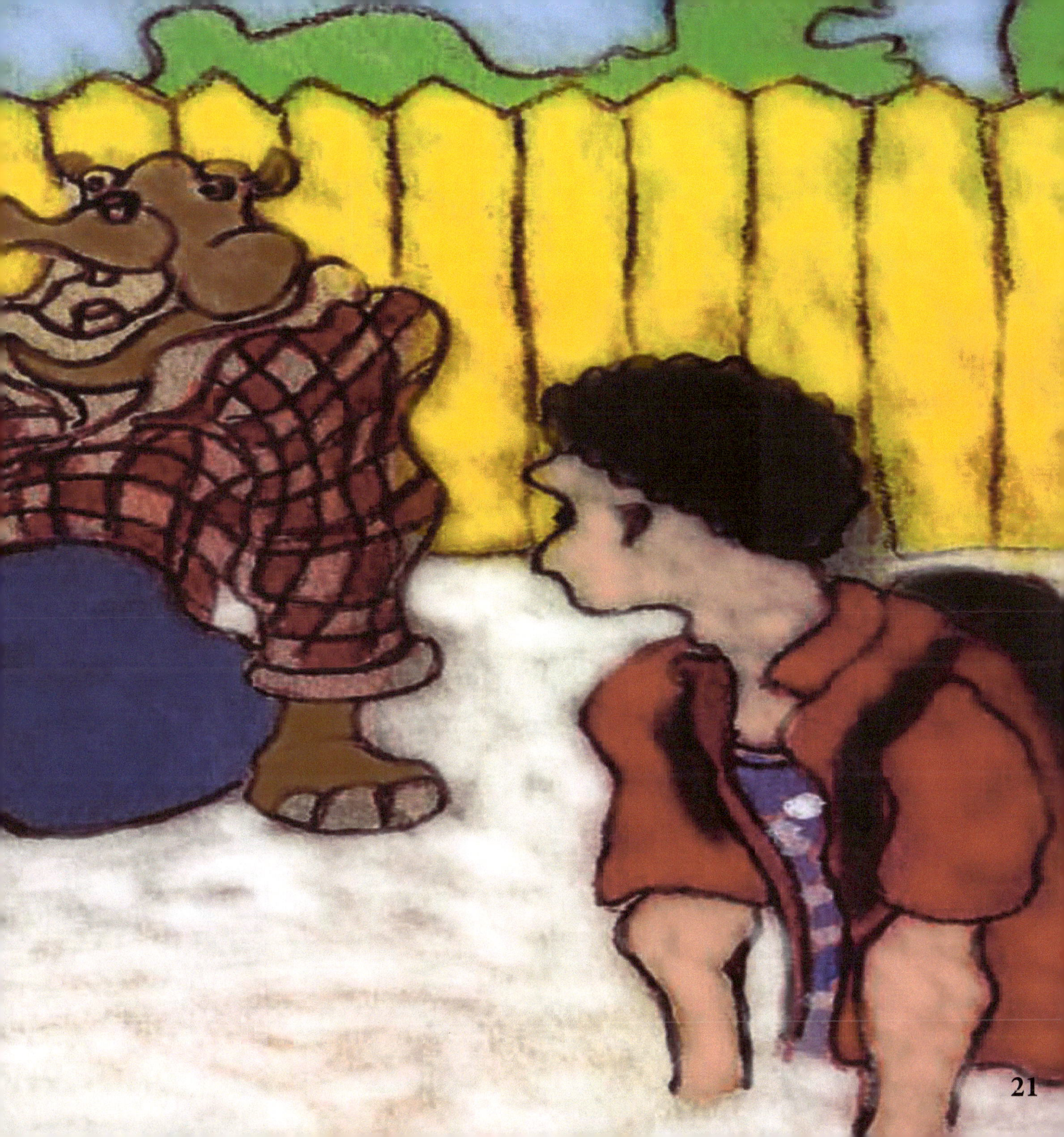

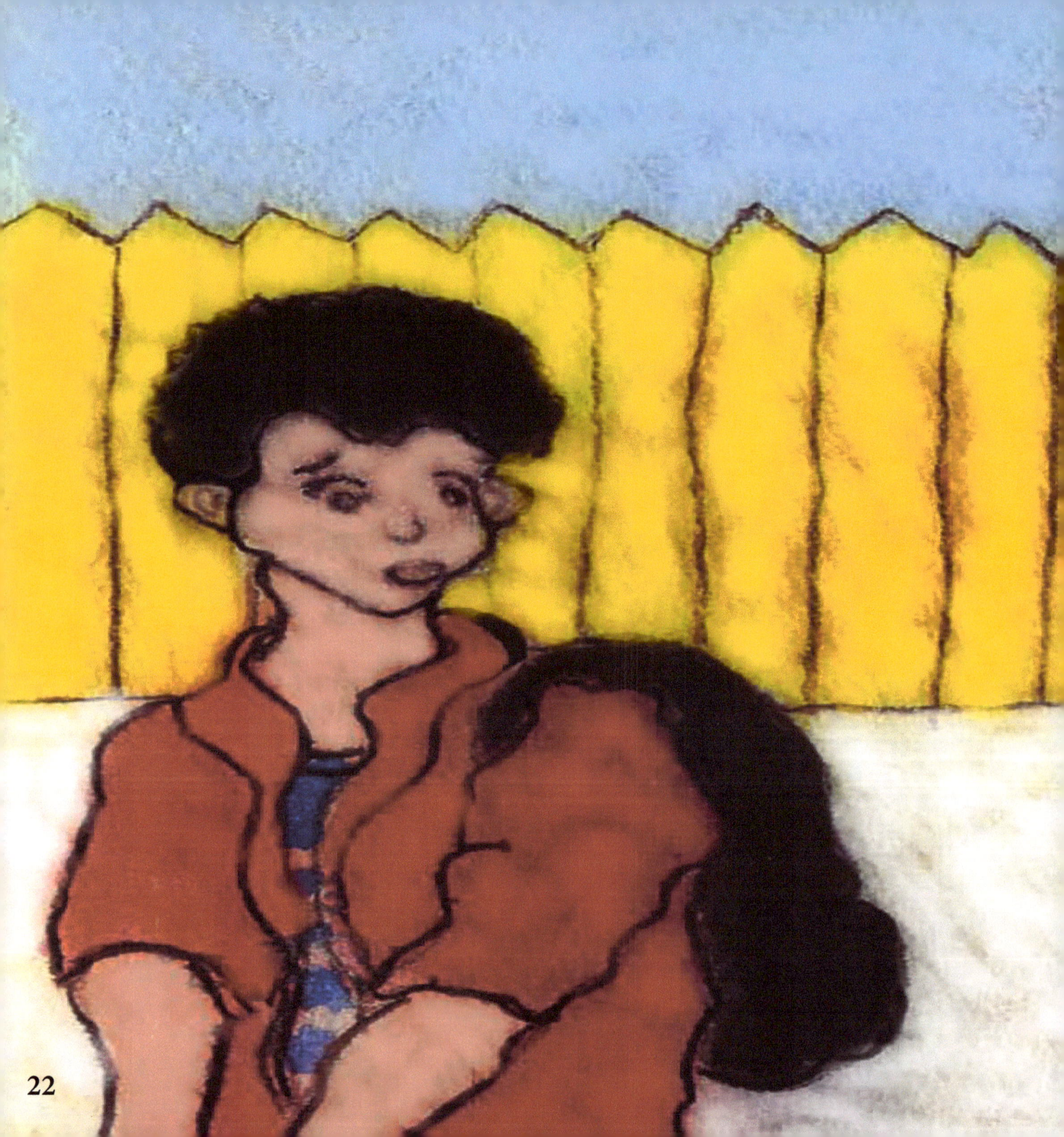

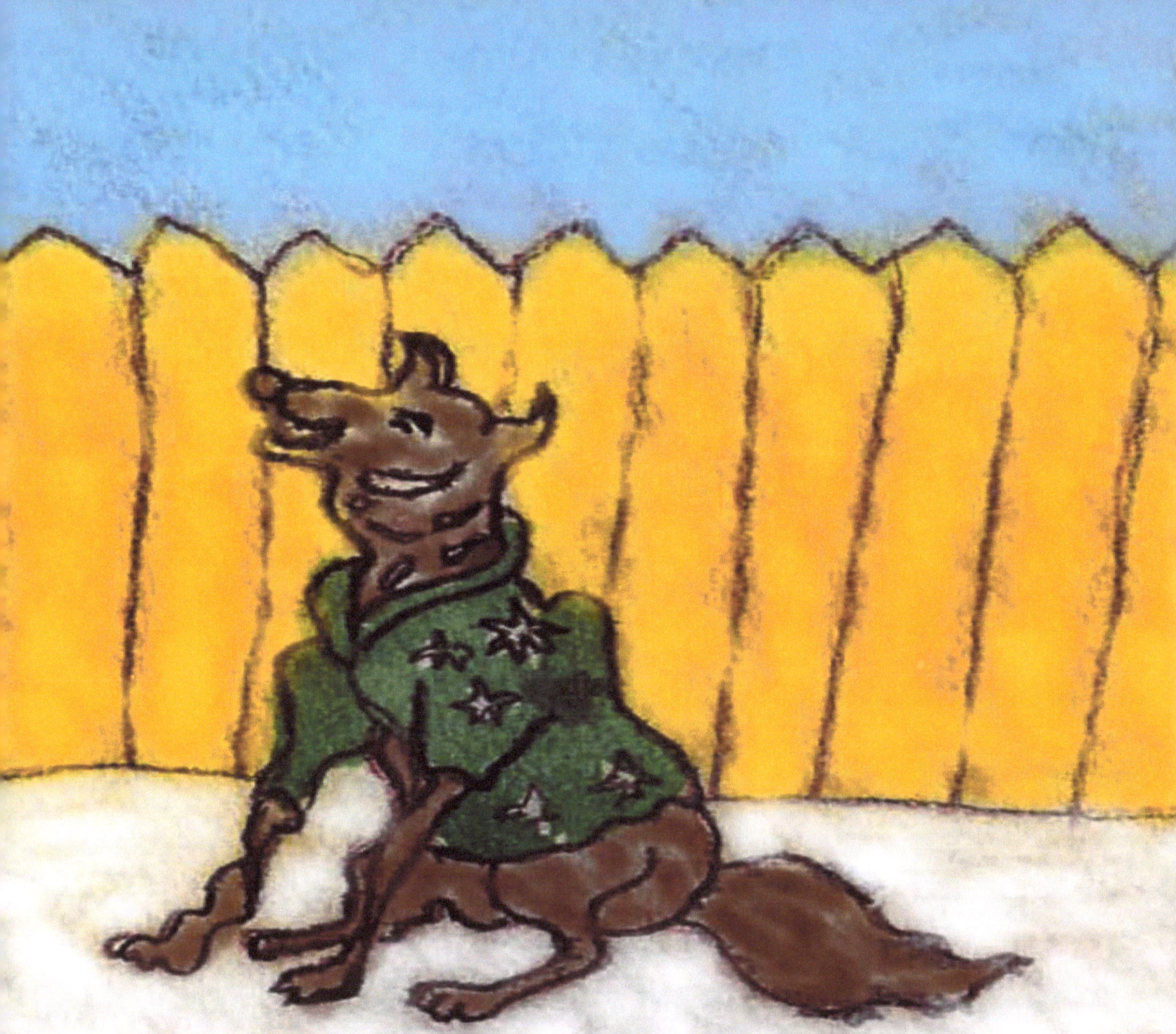

A hyena came by looking up, just laughing at the clear blue sky... but I did not laugh, oh no, not I! I just wanted to cry, **"SOMETHING IS MISSING."**

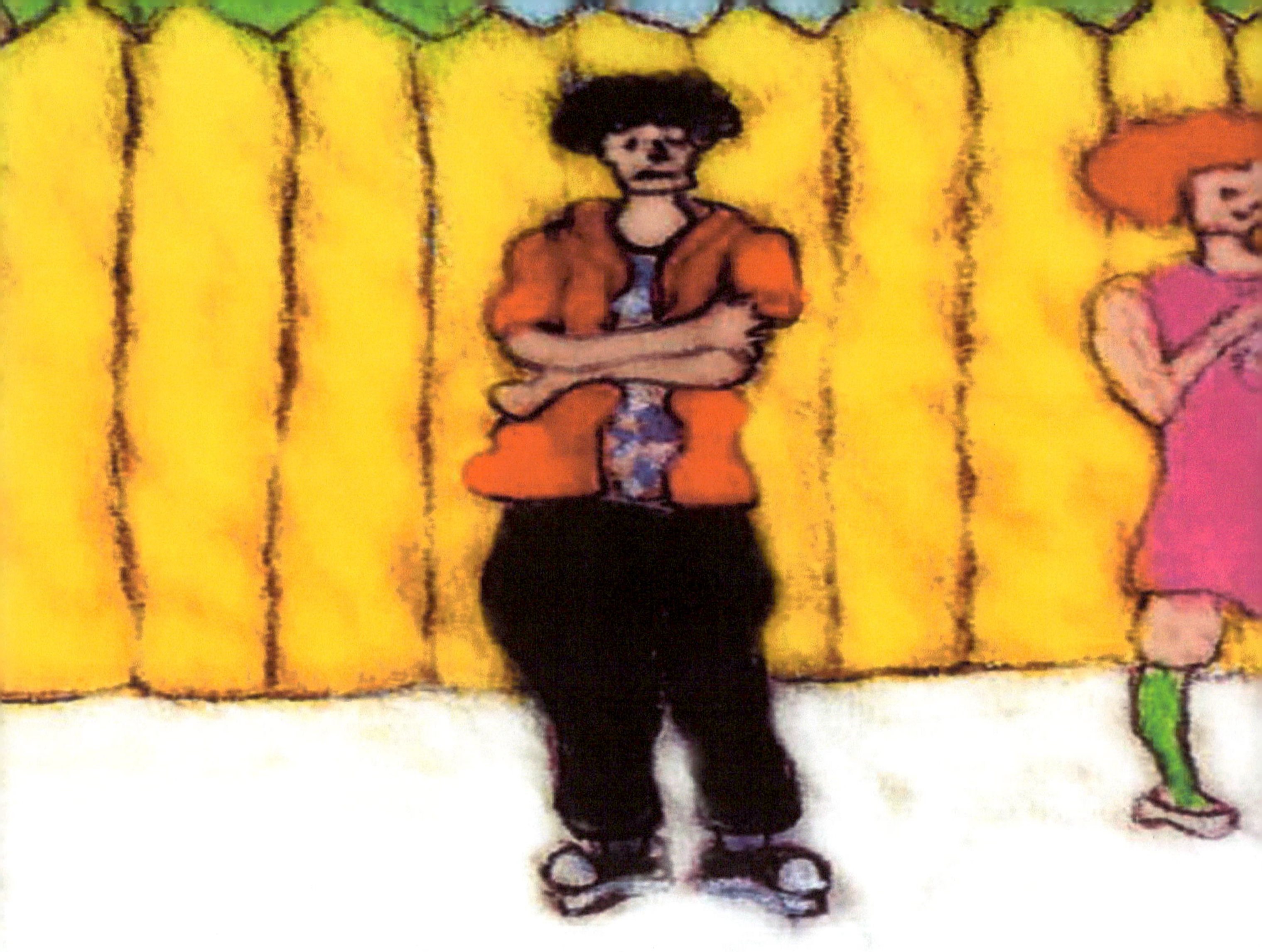

A llama came and danced with a chimpanzee, and that was a sight to see. Everyone laughed, but not me. No laughing for me. Nothing was funny to me you see, I just wanted to cry, **"SOMETHING IS MISSING."**

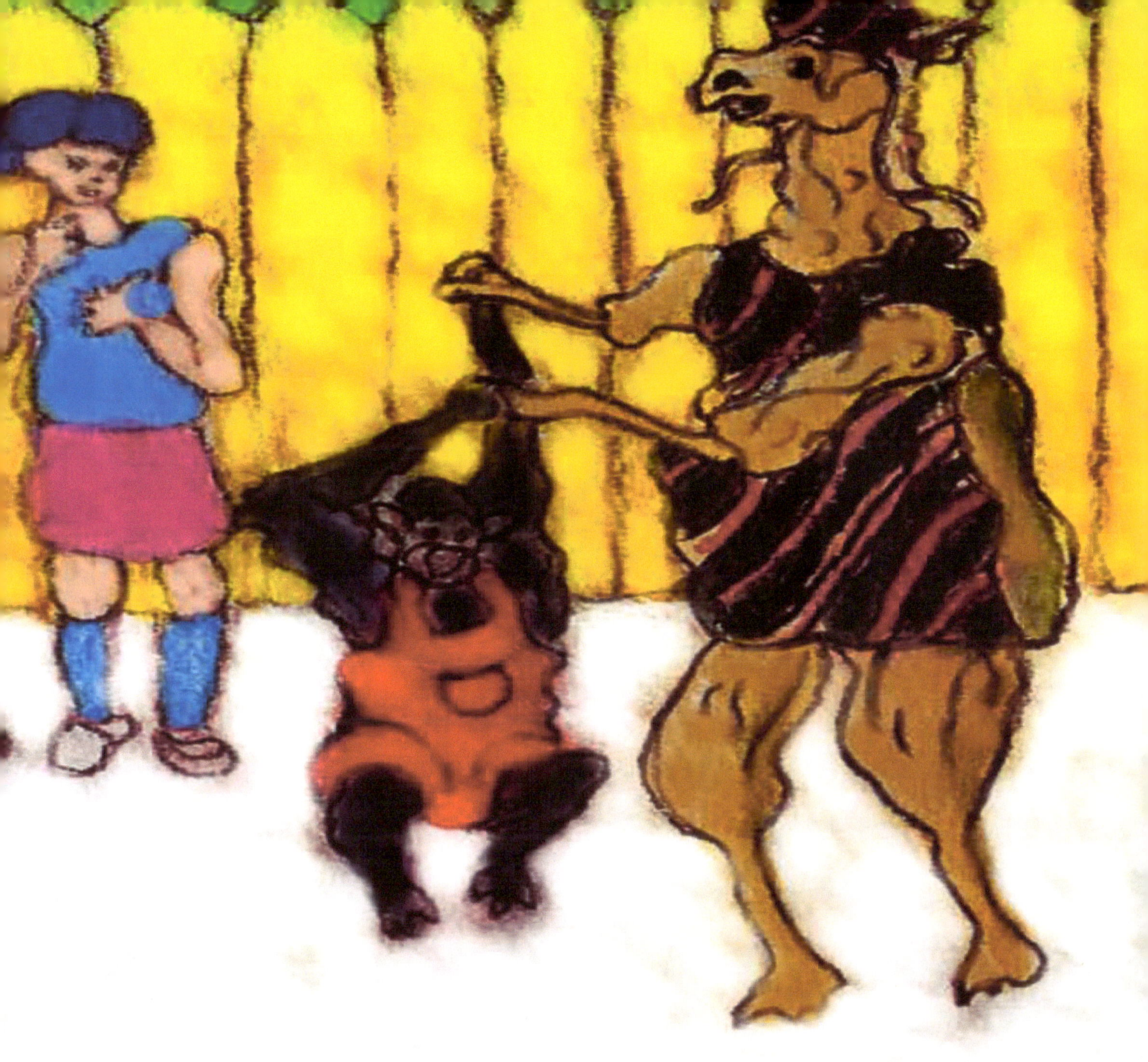

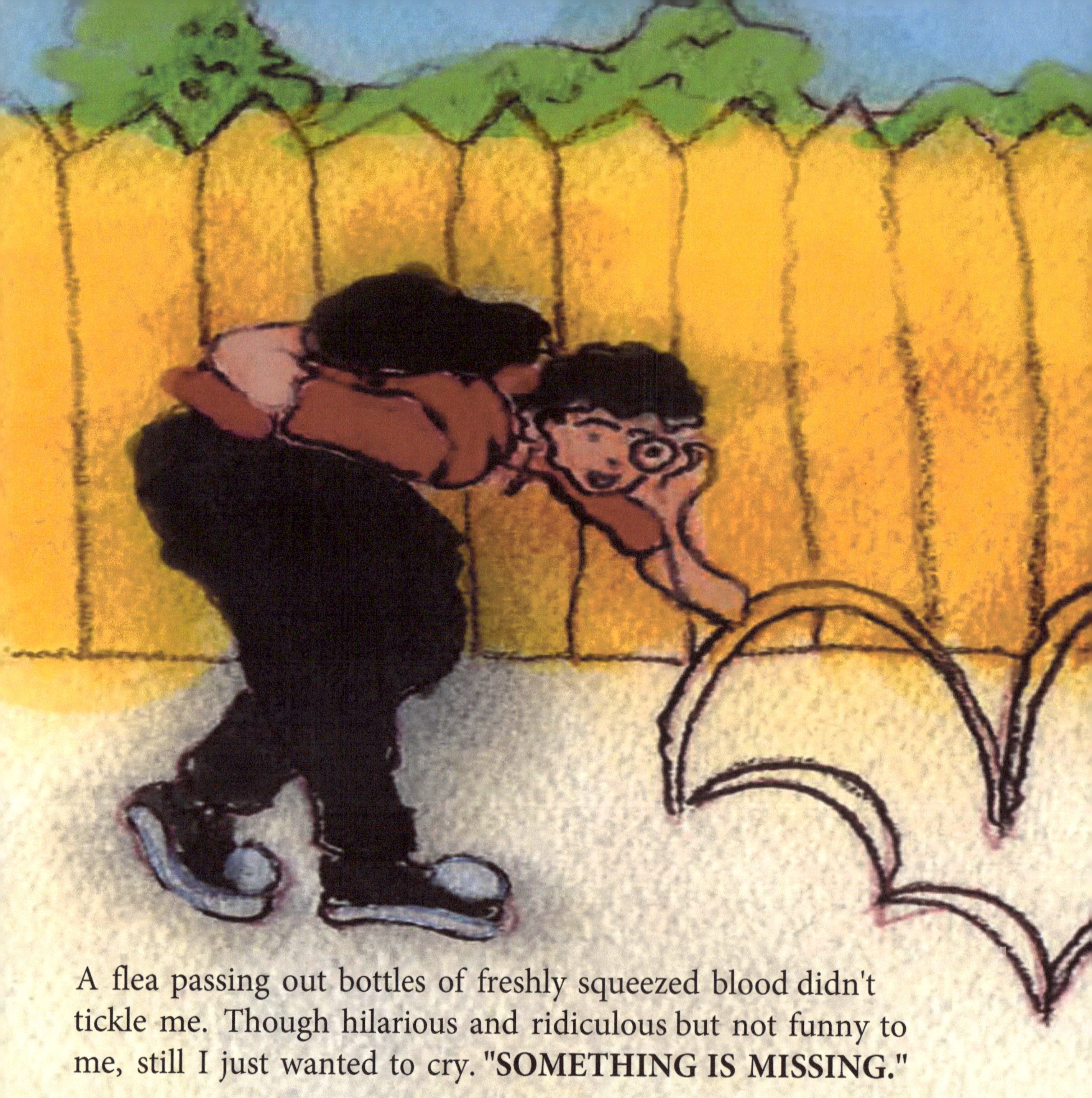

A flea passing out bottles of freshly squeezed blood didn't tickle me. Though hilarious and ridiculous but not funny to me, still I just wanted to cry. **"SOMETHING IS MISSING."**

26

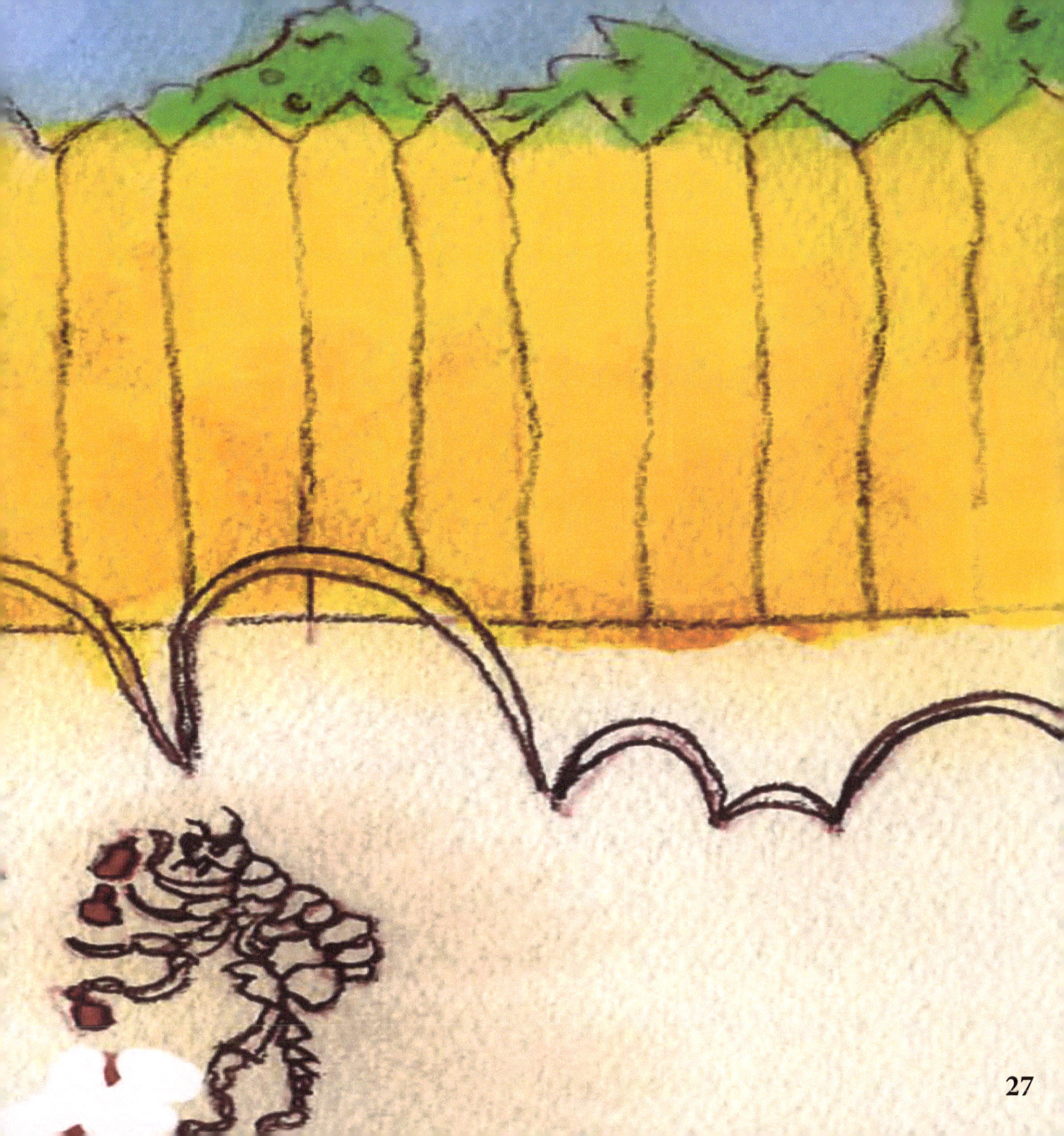

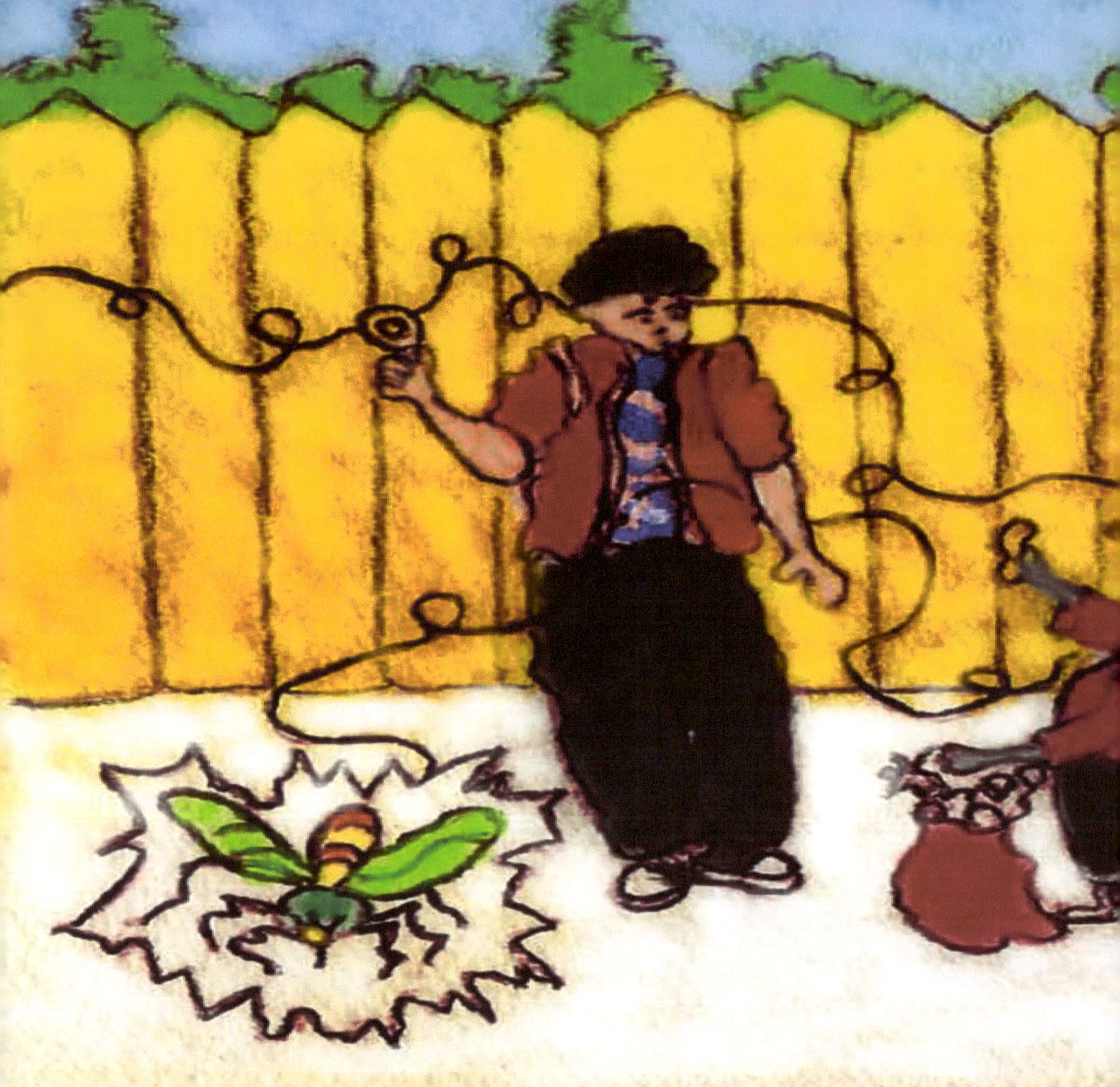

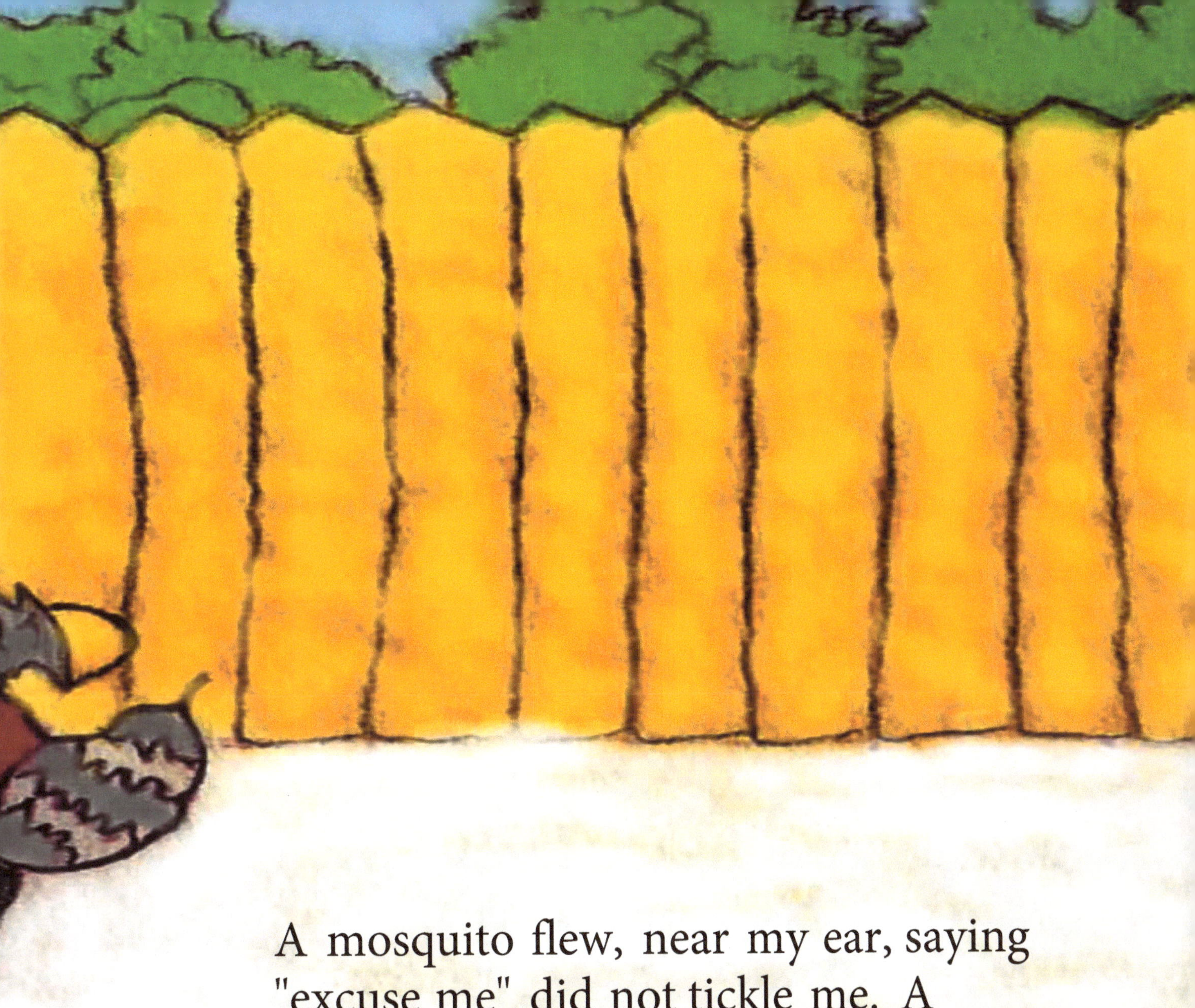

A mosquito flew, near my ear, saying
"excuse me" did not tickle me. A
raccoon bringing back what he had
stolen the night before. My! my! but
this sight did not fancy my tickle delight.

I could not understand that with all of this happening with everyone else laughing, I just wanted to cry, until out of nowhere a flying fish came and sat across the street from me eating the bone that the rottweiler was to afraid to retrieve or take back. I just wanted to cry. **"SOMETHING IS MISSING."**

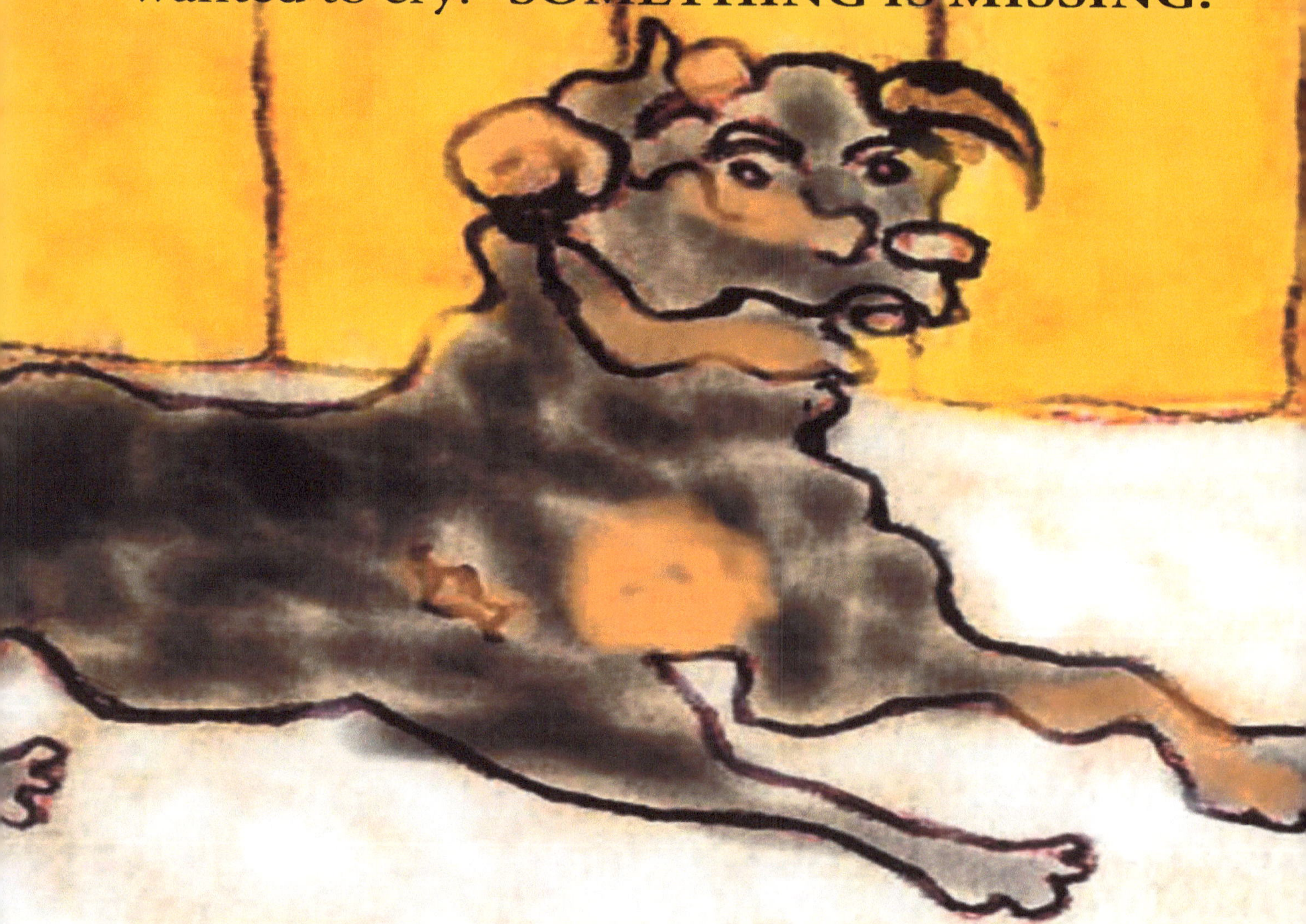

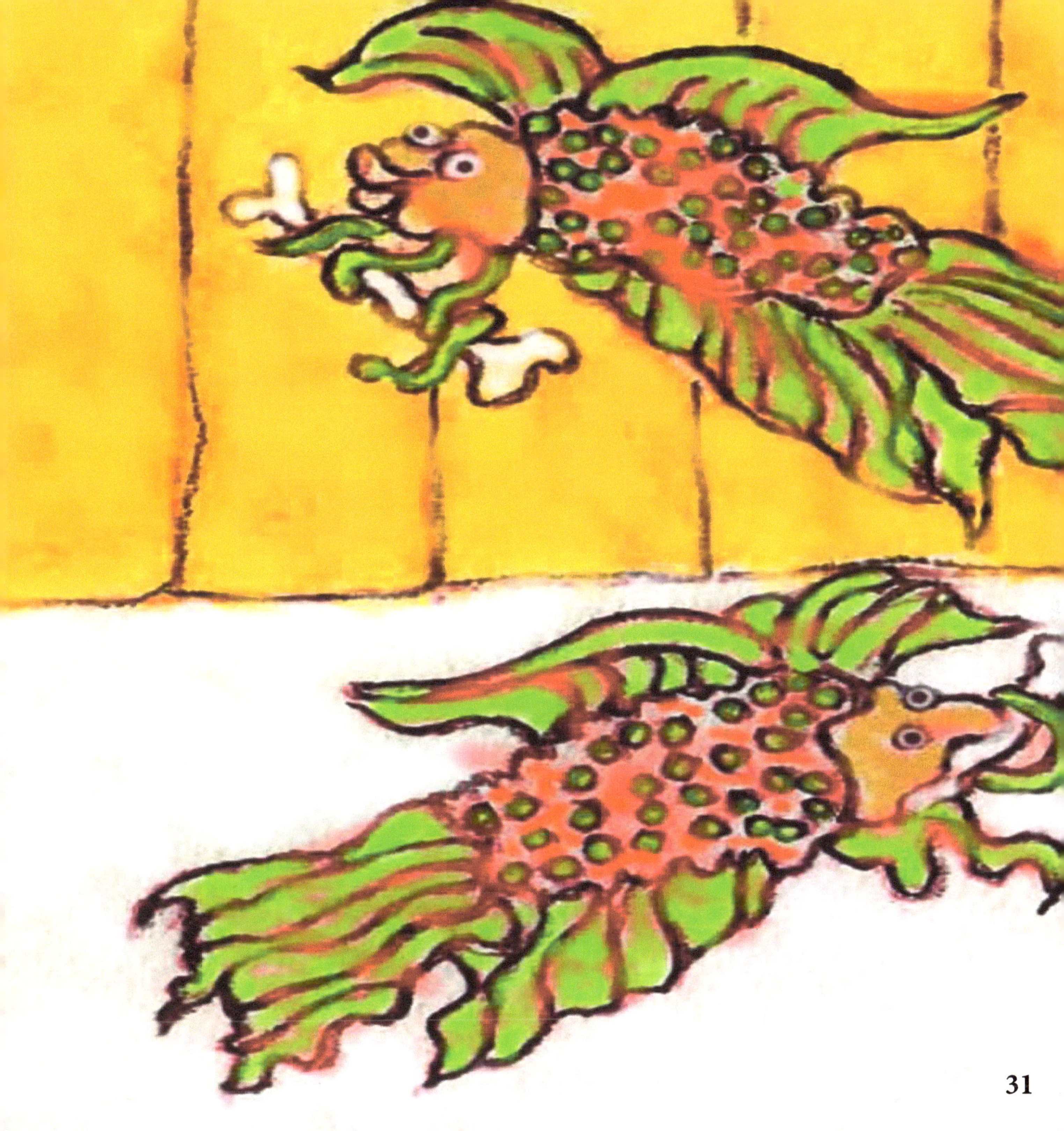

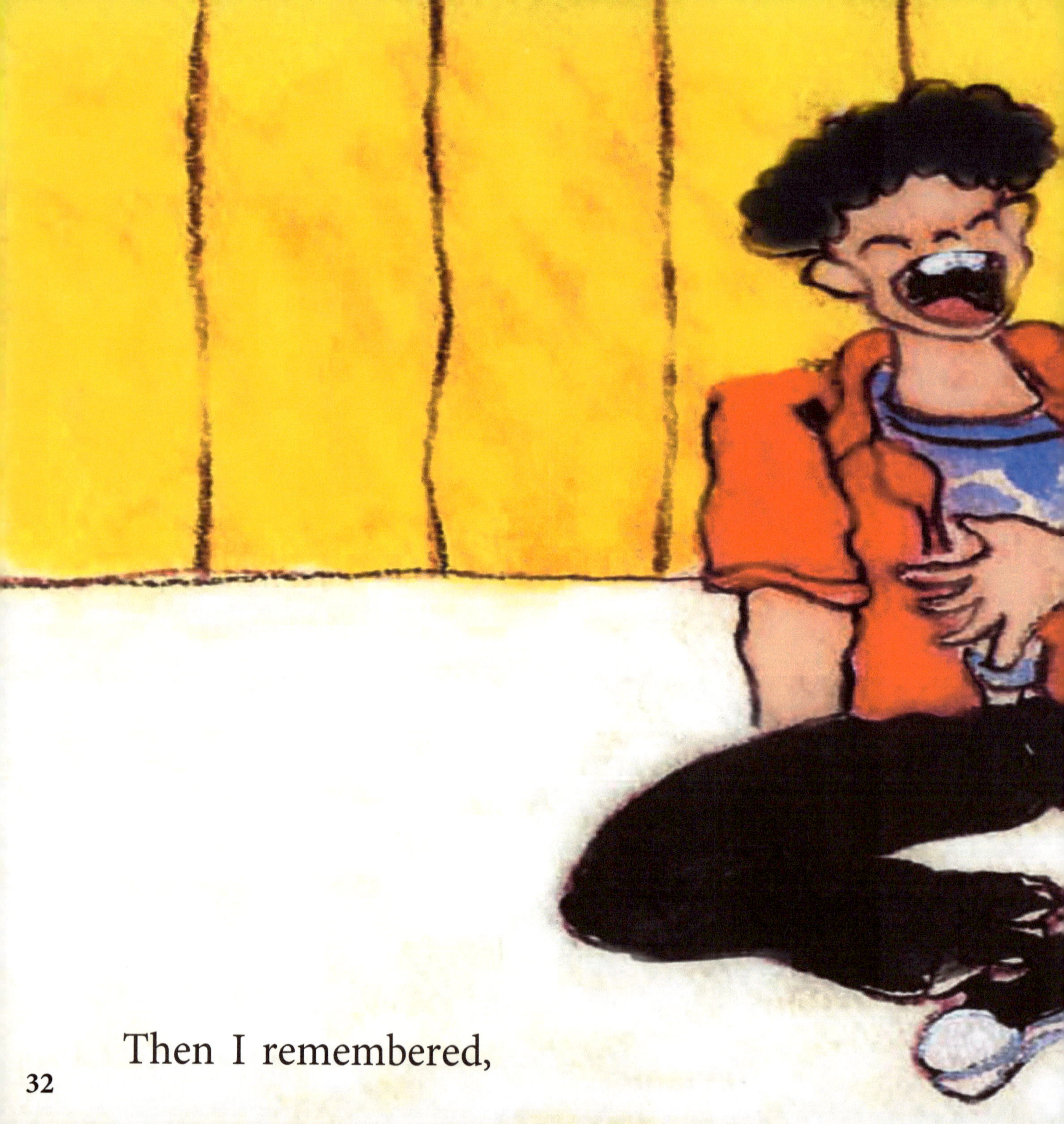

Then I remembered,

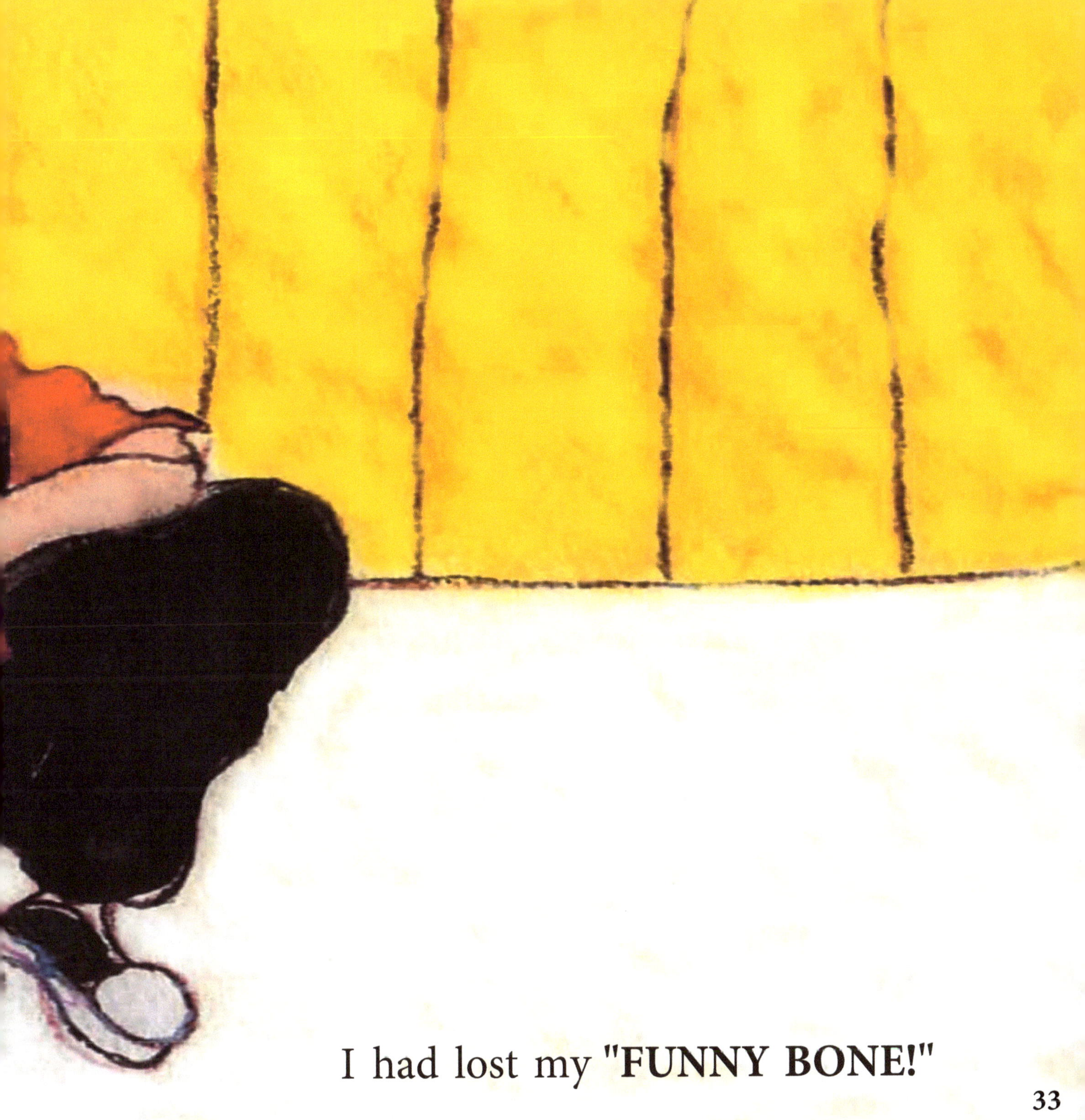

I had lost my **"FUNNY BONE!"**

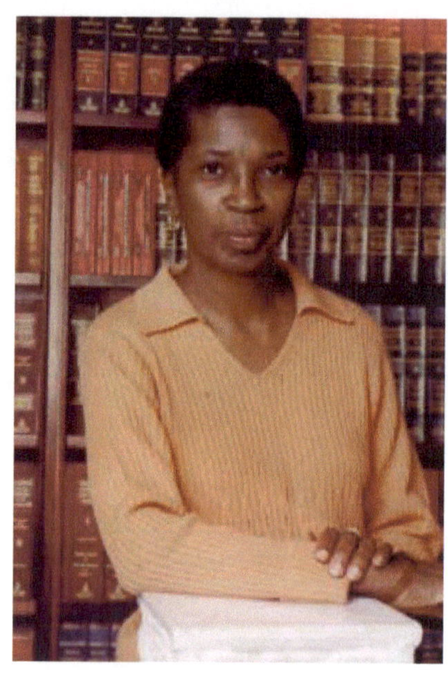

About the Author

Christine Olufemi, an educator, poet, and the
mother of three adult children resides in Atlanta, Ga.
She is open to creative expressions that help to engage
the reading audience's interest.

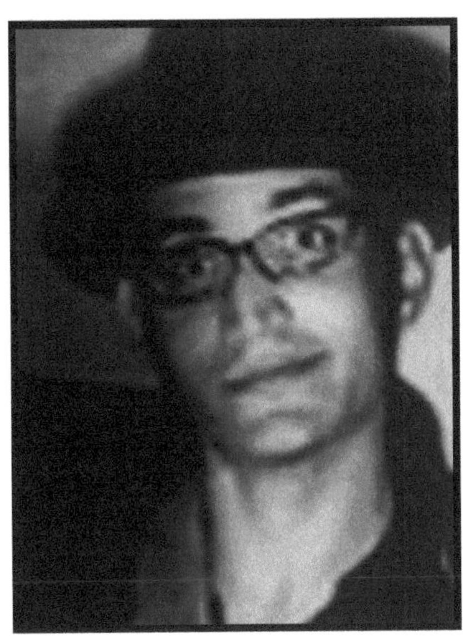

About the Artist

Pedro Luis Rivas, an artist, illustrator native from the Dominican Republic, resides in Atlanta, Ga. He is a graduate from the Portfolio Center with a Degree in Illustration and Graphic design, his multicultural experiences are always present in his work with the goal of communicating to all races the message of unity through his artwork and personal experiences.

 www.ingramcontent.com/pod-product-compliance
Lightning Source LLC
Chambersburg PA
CBHW042203030726
47602CB00007B/103